Glowing Comments from Leaders about...

Yes! —How Noes Prepare You
for the Yeses that Shape Your Future

John Fuhrman

"Enthusiasm is contagious, and Yes! *is worth catching."*

—ANNETTE SYKORA, IMMEDIATE PAST CHAIRPERSON,
NATIONAL AUTO DEALERS ASSOCIATION
AND OWNER OF SEVERAL DEALERSHIPS

"Say Yes to Yes! *John Fuhrman's lessons and philosophies apply to an individual's pursuit of a more fulfilling life as adeptly as they do toward the pursuit of sales and marketing excellence. This is truly an inspirational read for all."*

—STAN STARNES, PRESIDENT
SERVICE CONTRACT SALES DIVISION
DENT ZONE COMPANIES

"John's book, Yes!, *is a breath of fresh air in the world of leadership. His advice is touching and insightful, and makes me want to truly focus on mentoring others. My entire dissertation was on mentorship and this book inspired me to more effectively reach out to others in the field."*

—DR. PAULA KENNEDY-DUDLEY
DIRECTOR OF STUDENT SERVICES, SCHOOL OF NURSING
UNIVERSITY OF NORTH CAROLINA AT WILMINGTON

"John has written another masterpiece in personal growth. Yes! *is a fascinating and insightful interpretation of two simple words we use every day. After reading this book, you may never look at yes and no in the same way."*

—CAROLYN KINDLEY-SINGLE
BROKER/FOUNDER/CERTIFIED MENTOR
GREEN PARACHUTE, LLC

"Congratulations on a great read! You remind us of the importance of staying positive; having a plan. I liked the way you interweaved personal experiences to illustrate various points. Thanks for sharing Yes!"

—MICHAEL MCHUGH
SENIOR VICE PRESIDENT OF SALES
GMAC INSURANCE

The Road to Yes Begins When YOU Say Yes!

Dear Reader,

John Fuhrman is where he is in life because he looks at "no" a bit differently than most. His success is definitely not due to avoiding no. It's the result of realizing no exists, embracing it as an opportunity to learn, grow, and achieve yes! Your results, the yeses and noes, and your subsequent responses to them, have brought you to your current station in life as well.

Unfortunately, most people shy away from no and the potential of failing. While this may provide immediate, short-term comfort, it prevents any possibility of achieving desires beyond the ordinary. The only way we can earn the yeses that truly shape our lives is to be open to the noes and failings that we encounter along the way. Accept them as necessary bumps in the road to where you're going. Even though it's paved with no, follow your path in spite of any fear you may have. No is overcome simply by saying yes, over and over again, to your dream, goal, or objective—no matter what challenges come your way.

Had John not been willing to subject himself to the many noes he received in response to his book proposals, along with countless rewrites, he would never have been published—*nine times now!* It wasn't that he set out wanting to hear no and fail, but rather that he was willing to receive a hundred noes to get one yes. I can assure you he never enjoyed a single no. No way! Every one was met with a certain amount of resistance to the truth, as well as tension, self-doubt, and anger. But that one yes he got from us led to a new career as a popular author and speaker! John will tell you every no was worth more than he ever could have ever imagined.

John soon realized that no indicated the need to make changes, grow, and improve his approach in order to enhance his chances for yes. Had he kept doing the same old things in the same old ways he would have gotten the same old results—noes—rather than the new and exciting yeses he was after.

Had John submitted his initial rough manuscript to us here at Possibility Press, the publisher who finally said yes, there's little chance we would have given it a second glance. As he got no after no, he was told that, while the ideas were there they were poorly organized and written. His success as an author is the direct result of making changes and improvements in response to the noes he was continually receiving from other publishers. This principle is essential for success in every area of life. If at first you're getting no, take heart and press on—you're on the right track to getting yes!

No one does everything exactly right the first time they do something new. Those who eventually get yes are those who risked getting no—making adjustments and improvements as they went. They didn't quit on themselves or anyone else.

Successful people are always open to no and failure. They realize it's the fastest way to improve and get yes. People who choose to do something new typically don't know much at first about how they're going to do it! They learn how as they go, asking for help as needed, and grow—moving forward toward their new objective. They understand that *the answer to how is yes!*

Those who avoid no while convincing themselves, and maybe even others, that they're still "working on it," will never feel quite ready. Some toil for years trying to create perfection or make their efforts "no-proof." But that just doesn't work. It simply doesn't enable progress. The only thing that works is going forward in the face of no.

A few years ago, after the remarkable success of John's first book, *Reject Me—I Love It!*, he was asked to speak at a writers' conference. It was a group of authors with manuscripts at various stages of development. Some were finished, while others hadn't written a single word! One writer, in particular, paid incredibly close attention to everything John said, taking copious notes on every aspect of the session.

Four years later, John ran into him again at another conference. Guess what? He was *still* working on his first book. He said it wasn't ready yet. He was rewriting it for the umpteenth time, never believing it was good enough. When John suggested submitting it to a publisher to test the waters, his answer surprised John. He said there was no way he could survive being told no once, let alone as many times as John had. He wasn't going to submit anything until it was, in his opinion, "no-proof."

Since John's first book was published, eight more have been released, while the no-proof writer is still rewriting his first! Furthermore, John's books have also been published in over a dozen other languages as well. As John says, "Who would've thunk it?" The perfectionist's finished product could potentially be an epic for all time, but we'll probably never get to read it because he believes it's never going to be ready!

John can't change the fact that over a hundred publishers told him no. However, in every single case, each time he sent out a proposal he believed it to be better than the previous one. He was confident the next publisher would be the one who would say yes and accept it. He never intentionally mailed something out expecting to get a no. Neither should you in your endeavors. Negative expectation will only set you up to get exactly that—a no!

Now John's not asking you to enjoy the noes. Nor is he asking you to give less than your all, believing you'll fail. His goal is to move you to action—to see you put forth your current best effort, better it as you proceed, and do whatever's required to get the desired result. The key to getting yes comes in *growing* through the noes—not just going through them. As you shall learn, it's not just a numbers game either. Adopt that idea, get in motion, and keep paving the road to yes so you can achieve whatever it is you desire.

No Isn't a Problem—*It's an Opportunity, and a Badge of Honor and Courage!*

Everyone wants to be accepted and told yes. But if we don't risk getting no, we can't grow personally, our income won't grow as we may want, and our life won't be as great as we'd like it to be. Getting noes isn't about whether people like you or not; it's about being humble and developing your skills. Never take no personally.

No isn't a problem; it's an opportunity to develop your skills and become more of who you'd like to be! No is a chance for you to grow and do more of what you'd like to do. No is a step on the path to be rewarded with more of what you'd like to have—experiences, relationships, more control of your time, increased income—whatever you're seeking.

Have you ever offered anyone a bottle of water or a cup of coffee or tea and they said "No thanks"? Was that devastating? Did it hurt you? Of course not! You probably didn't think anything of it. Right? Have you ever said, "No thanks," when someone offered you something? Sure! Can you see no in a different light now?

This book shares some of the wisdom John has gained through his own no experiences, as well as those of others who have risked no in their quest for yes. If he hadn't grown through more challenges, and more noes, since his last book, *Leading Leaders to Leadership*, he simply wouldn't have had anything more to share. There would have been no reason for his writing *Yes!* nor us publishing it.

If you don't experience more noes, whether in person, from the media, or over the Internet, you won't grow and achieve the success you want either. Naysayers are a dime a dozen, and they have nothing to offer but sour grapes. They probably aren't very successful and they don't want you to be very successful either! Yes, jealousy still exists.

Getting and growing through no is the *only* way to success! No doubt about it. It's the key. Most people either just don't seem to understand this or they refuse to. They see the achievements of others alright, but what's visible is only the tip of an iceberg built on countless submerged noes and other challenges overcome.

No opens the doors to new knowledge and experiences you otherwise wouldn't have gained. No prepares you to find and walk confidently with yes. No will take you to places you never imagined and help you achieve more success than you ever felt possible—as long as you persist.

As you move along in your quest for yes, remember these key points:

- Never take no personally or as the ultimate answer.
- The road to yes is paved with no.
- No is for you to grow, preparing you for yes.
- Winners don't quit when they get a no—it only makes them stronger and more determined.

Yes creates a new set of opportunities, while no strengthens you for them. Embrace noes for what they teach, while helping you grow so you can attract and best serve the yeses. Thank the noes, smiling to yourself, for they save you from wasting time on negative situations.

Now get out there and see how many noes you can get; each one presents its own special gifts, pushing you to grow—in exciting ways you probably can't even imagine. Remember, no is an opportunity. Wear it as a badge of honor and courage!

Get ready for the yeses that shape your future. Hear no and keep going and growing, and you'll be heading for yes and the top. Use *Yes!* to play a positive role in helping you create the kind of success you so desire.

YES! to your success,

The Publisher

Yes!

How Noes Prepare You for the Yeses that Shape Your Future

John Fuhrman

Bestselling Author of *Leading Leaders to Leadership*

A Possibility Press **Book**

Yes!

John Fuhrman

Copyright © 2010 by John Fuhrman
ISBN 978-0-938716-71-6

Published by
Possibility Press
possibilitypress.com

Manufactured in the United States of America

Dedication

To all the people who told me no: Thanks! You've caused me to grow and become better than I ever could have imagined, enabling me to live my dream.

To the dreamers who are becoming greater doers: Face no with courage and conviction, knowing it'll move you closer toward living *your* dream.

Acknowledgment

When I think of all the people and things that influenced my life and the directions it has taken, I can't help but thank them. Where I am now in life is the sum total of everything that has happened to me and what I did as a result. Had I been protected from no and failure, or conditioned to simply accept it, few of the things I am thankful for in life would have happened.

I thank the speaker's bureaus and event planners who have invited me to share my message with their audiences. You've helped keep me going as a writer. Thank you for telling me what you want.

To all the supporters of this project, a special thanks. I wanted this book to be special and you all kept me believing it would be. Thanks also to the editors who polished it up to make it better than I ever hoped it could have been. I will forever be in your debt for helping me send a needed message to those who want to grow.

A special thanks to family and friends who understood, from the beginning, that sacrificing time then would give us the freedom to enjoy more time together now. I look forward to sharing the joys life has brought me, teaching the lessons I've learned.

Finally, thanks to all of you who aren't quite sure if you can live the life you've always dreamed of. You helped spur me on to do this book. For much of my life I've walked in your shoes, shared your doubts, had your fears. But because people were willing to share with me what I hope you'll see in this book, I now live my dreams. I hope I'm an example of what your life can be as well.

are chosen for the picks to practice with. With each passing round, the odds increase monumentally against ever being on the field of a major league ballpark.

What do you suppose the odds would be if you were chosen after all the teams had picked 50 players? How about 60? That would mean after 50 or 60 complete rounds of choosing, you may not even have been seriously thought of! Now suppose, in the 62nd and final round, on the last pick by the last team, they called your name—and then only as a favor to your father!

In 1988, that pick actually occurred. The father was a friend of then-manager of the Dodgers, Tommy Lasorda, and they chose a catcher who would certainly rise above the odds. So much so, that he would surely be destined to be voted into baseball's highest society—the Hall of Fame. His name? Mike Piazza. And even though he's actually number five on my list, his quote is the best at summing up what no and failing, and yes and succeeding, are all about: "I'm not trying to prove anybody wrong. I'm just trying to prove something to myself."

Forget Realistic—*Believe the Impossible Can Happen!*

It was the summer of 1969 when our world seemed to dramatically shrink. We suddenly saw just how small and fragile it looked when viewed from the moon. After taking "One small step for man, one giant leap for mankind," astronaut Neil Armstrong placed one foot onto the lunar surface. Many of us who saw it on TV instantly thought of an earlier time.

In April 1961, a certain man had affirmed this would happen. Even though we hadn't yet developed a rocket that could get us there, he said we would do it. Before the technology was developed to make such a trip possible, he insisted we'd achieve it. Without even having any trained and qualified people to make the trip, he had the foresight to insist this would be a reality. Who would say such a thing? Was he a psychic?

No, he was John F. Kennedy, President of the United States. At a time when the country needed to be inspired, he ventured beyond the known. He dared to be unrealistic, to believe in the impossible. Most importantly, though, he *insisted* it be done. Kennedy didn't predict the moon landing; he simply stated that it would be done by the end of the decade. He never paid attention to the naysayers who said, "It can't be done." That would have been fatal to his mission. How about you?

Kennedy's proclamation made a great impact on me, teaching me the power of positive certainty. There was never a sense of maybe, perhaps, or try in his voice—only clarity, strength, and faith—never waffling or wavering. All of my goals started the same way with "We Will..." or rather "I Will...." How about yours? Are you saying, "No Excuse! I'm Doing It," as Jay Rifenbary does in his bestselling book?

Those who've accomplished something new didn't know exactly how they were going to do it when they began, other than maybe having a basic idea. They went forward with the positive certainty that they'd attain their aspiration, driving themselves to learn how to do it on the way to accomplishing it. They learned a basic truth...

...The Answer to How Is *Yes!*

Knowing why you're here, where you truly belong, and what works best for you can go a long way toward building a successful, satisfying life. Just know that preparing for that success by doing things differently from your family, friends, neighbors, and acquaintances—and, perhaps, doing better than they have done—can cause challenges. Not to be concerned. This is common for anyone who ventures out.

When his opportunity to compete in the Olympics finally came, he felt prepared. His training, done mostly on his own, had been different than the traditional approach. Nevertheless, his history of winning performances made him a favorite for victory. However, as so often happens, due to the many dynamics of life, things beyond his control entered the scene and changed the situation.

Due to a scheduling change, he was forced to participate in a race without being able to rest from the previous one. In spite of this, though, he managed a fourth-place among the world's top runners. Still, the press discounted his accomplishment, blaming his failing to take first place entirely on his having rejected traditional training methods.

To redeem himself, he decided to show them simply by breaking the world's record! He resolved to achieve a mark that had never been accomplished before. This would all take place while he was studying medicine, allowing him to train only 45 minutes a day. Nevertheless, he was convinced that deliberate, steady training would enable him to accomplish his goal. He knew the answer to how was yes!

With friends who ran with him in support of his quest, he entered the competition. After just four quarter-mile laps, he broke the tape and the "insurmountable" mark. The stopwatch read an incredible 3:59.4! Six tenths of a second less than the four-minute mark the world said couldn't be broken! Roger Bannister not only broke the world record; a couple of months later he broke it again by nearly another second. Curiously, as soon as this so-called impossible time had been attained, other runners began breaking the four-minute mile "barrier" as well.

As is typically the case, barriers are creations of the mind, false beliefs. Just say yes and make it so. When asked about his choice of races, Sir Roger Bannister replied, "I found longer races boring. The mile was just perfect."

Kicked Out of Your Own Country

Sometimes, no matter how good an idea is, few may be open-minded enough to listen. You might have to leave your hometown or your country just to have a chance. As the expression goes, "You're not a prophet in your own land." You're just good ol' you to them. People close to you may have preconceived notions about you and may well take you for granted. Even though you're growing, they can't see or understand it if they're not. If they know you've changed, they may not like it. It's sad they don't realize we all need to change on the inside to create the change we want on the outside.

Now here's a guy I'd love to have on my sales team. Christopher Columbus had colossal setbacks, kept going and, even after a final huge mistake, still achieved greatness. After failing to get his Italian homeland to sanction a voyage designed to prove the earth was round, he left for Spain. Then after doing some serious convincing to Queen Isabella, he was commissioned to go out and search for a more direct route to the Far East to increase trade. Since there were no maps to guide him, he failed—massively. The result—he found America! Out of all the noes came a giant YES. Columbus never bought into the popular belief that the earth was flat. In taking the risk that he would fall off the end of it, he discovered a whole new world.

Not bad for hearing no but refusing to quit. Christopher Columbus proved that continuing to follow a passionate dream can result in success beyond imagination. He went to what could have been his demise to make his objective a reality. For that, most people might have him as number one. However, the following man set out with a specific purpose, which is why he's my number one choice.

Don't Stick Me with That!

Accidents happen. That's a fact of life. Success can also happen by accident but don't confuse this with luck. So-called accidental success really occurs when you're actively striving to accomplish something, working toward a definite goal. When you're in the arena doing something to the absolute best of your ability, that's when *it* happens.

Art Fry was a member of his church's choir. During the week, he worked for a company called 3M where he had been since he graduated from college. To promote synergy, the company's leaders always encouraged employees to think and step outside their comfort zones.

Art learned about one of their scientists, Spencer Silver, and his failed attempts, four years earlier, at finding a stronger adhesive. Silver had developed a new compound, but it proved to be weaker than what 3M was already producing. You'd think that a company known for making Scotch Tape® and other great adhesives would have a use for one that could stick to various items, yet easily be lifted off and be reused. But no one knew what to do with it. However, Art had a challenge at church—where he thought the new adhesive might work.

He kept losing his place whenever he used standard book-marks in the hymnals during services. Frustrated, he took some of Silver's adhesive and applied it to the back of a bookmark. Much to his surprise, he found it would stick to a page and stay put, yet could be easily moved to another page without damaging the first. Incredibly, the bookmark with the four-year-old adhesive retained sufficient stickiness even after several applications and removals.

Then, one day at work, Art used one of his new bookmarks to make a note, sticking it to a report. Other employees saw how it worked, and shortly thereafter Art was inundated with requests for some of his semi-sticky notepaper.

Because of a failed experiment four years earlier, and the quest to solve a non-work-related problem, you've come to know Art's creation by its world-famous name—Post-It® Notes. He "stuck" with his belief, creating one of the handiest little products of all time, now sold in more than a hundred countries. Another no had been turned into a giant YES.

Fry was promoted to corporate scientist, the highest level an employee could receive on the technical side of 3M. In 1985, *Time* magazine said Post-It® Notes was one of the best products of the previous twenty-five years. Revenue from it and its spin-offs exceed $1 billion annually!

Hearing No and Failing Is Essential to *Hearing Yes and Succeeding*

If you've ever been told no (who hasn't?), you're in good company. Anyone who's accomplished anything of note has been told no somewhere along the line. They took no as a positive, using it to spur them on. Here's just a small list of some of those people and what they've accomplished:

- Bill Gates and Paul Allen, co-founders of Microsoft.
- Jeff Bezos, founder of Amazon.com.
- Sam Walton, founder of WalMart.
- Thomas Edison, inventor of the electric light and 1092 other things.
- Madame Curie, discoverer of radium.
- Eli Witney, inventor of the cotton gin.
- Robert Fulton, developer of commercially successful steamboats.
- Abraham Lincoln, sixteenth President of the U.S.
- Winston Churchill, a former Prime Minister of Great Britain.
- Ludwig von Beethoven, deaf composer.
- Charles Goodyear, developer of the vulcanization of rubber.
- Mohandas Gandhi, agent of India's freedom.
- William Durant, founder of General Motors.
- Henry Ford, developer of the assembly line.
- Alexander Graham Bell, inventor of the telephone.
- Dr. Martin Luther King, Jr., founder of the civil rights movement.
- Thomas Watson, founder of IBM.
- Edison de Castro, founder of Data General.
- Steve Jobs and Steve Wozniak, founders of Apple Computer.
- Gail Borden, developer of evaporated milk.
- Jonas Salk, developer of the polio vaccine.
- Orville and Wilbur Wright, inventors of the airplane.
- Al Neuharth, creator of *USA Today*.
- Isaac Singer, inventor and promoter of the sewing machine.
- The list goes on and on and on.

These people—and countless others from all walks of life—had one thing in common that I hope will become more a part of you. In spite of being told no over and over again, they kept going. Committed to their quest, it just didn't matter what anyone else might have thought, said, or done to put them or what they were doing down. It just didn't matter if anyone tried to dissuade them. No only spurred them on to yes.

Hearing no and failing is essential to hearing yes and succeeding in any endeavor of any consequence. That you've heard no and have had some setbacks, yet you're steadfast in sticking to your aim, means you're moving forward toward something you're passionate about! It's something for which you're willing to risk repeatedly hearing no, until you get to the yeses that shape your future.

> *"The only person who never makes a mistake is the one who never does anything."*
>
> —THEODORE ROOSEVELT

The only thing separating you from your dreams and goals is whether you continue going for yes, or let no take control and stop you in your quest. It's hard to imagine a tiny two-letter word stopping anyone, isn't it? Come on now!

The proof is in the list. Whether you use my top five or your own favorites, the proof is right in front of you. Those who make it in life hear no and grow through it to yes. Just as in the dictionary, no and failure come before success. So, what are the key ingredients to yes? Consider this simple list:

- One part dream, goal, or objective.
- One part risk.
- One part effort.
- One part no.
- One part failing.
- Repeat as often as necessary to get yes.

The result? *Success!*

Now take a look at where you are in all areas of your life. Since you know the key ingredients for yes, simply identify which ones are missing from your life, add them in, and success is inevitable! That's just how it works.

"A great pleasure in life is doing what people say you cannot do."

—Walter Gagehot

1

Buying Into Yes or Selling Out to No?

Could you tell me how to do your job or business? Sure. However, knowing how to do a job or build and sustain a business has little to do with how successful the individual will be. The world is full of knowledgeable failures who know what to do, yet never totally apply themselves!

As a trainer and speaker, I've come across many people who are on the fast track to success. They're in a wide variety of fields and businesses, men and women from all over the world. Yet, I keep finding one common ingredient in each of them that seems to drive them to the top.

Long before they understood all the details of their chosen field, they went forward in faith with what they did know and were on their way. Even before they were taught and learned the nuances of their chosen jobs and businesses, something was pushing them to the top. Every one of them, without exception, said yes to themselves and knew *why* they were doing what they were doing. They had a purpose—a "WHY?" that was so important to them that they weren't concerned about the naysayers or noes they would get along the way. They saw no obstacles to achieving their objective.

They did everything with a result in mind. They knew why they were doing something rather than just knowing how to do it. You may be asking what the difference is since both can get the job done. But that's only part of the picture.

Do You Settle Just for What Comes Your Way?

Have you ever entered your home after a hard day at work and asked yourself what you did that day? You knew you went to work, did something that filled the hours of the day, then came home. Yet you have almost no memory of the details. Have you ever had a day like that? For some, it's like that almost every day.

You know them well. "So, so" is their battle cry. They often speak in terms of "what ifs" and "so whats." They work how they live—paycheck-to-paycheck—on the edge of financial disaster. Unfortunately, it doesn't even *seem* to bother them. They've somehow convinced themselves that they have security. But do they honestly look or feel secure? Or did they buy into a security illusion? What do you think?

People like that have fallen into what I call "settling in to settling for." Rather than risk losing the so-called security of a paycheck, they simply take whatever is given to them, rationalizing that they have plenty, are doing the best they can, or at least have enough to get by. When forced to do without, they tell themselves they didn't really need or want it anyway.

Some people might feel a little uncomfortable reading that. Still others may wonder how anyone could tolerate the ordinariness of that attitude, while creating a humdrum life. The sad thing is, 95 percent of working people make one of those decisions daily. They've seen what the majority has been doing, selling out to the illusion that they, too, must fall in line like everyone else.

They fail to observe that not venturing out and doing something different has led most people to bored complacency and feelings of being stuck. But must they remain in the stagnant frame of mind that's led to their stagnant circumstances? They sense discontent, but may not be confident enough that they can actually make a positive change that'll make a difference—they're that sure of failing. They're privately aware of their potential and unused ability, but refuse to cultivate it. Their fears magnify the risk, giving them an excuse to shy away from the possibilities.

This avoidance pattern controls their way of being, boxing them in to a life of routine repetition. Almost afraid of their own shadow, discouragement and depression often set in. This limited view of themselves might have been imposed on them as children by overcritical or over protective adults. Sadly, this attitude may be perpetuated by small-thinking people who don't want others to get ahead of them.

What Ifs Can Work Wonders

Suppose someone comes along, offering you an exciting alternative to the life you're living? Perhaps they show you a way to change it for the better, financially or personally, or better yet, both. Can you imagine yourself wondering, "What if this works? What if I could grow and become more than I am today? What if I could live the life I've always wanted"?

Or would you choose to maintain the status quo, justifying where you are, not accepting an offer to change and grow by saying, "I'm already where I want to be in life. My life's okay. I don't need to be any better than I am right now. This is as good as things are ever going to be for me"? People who offer that kind of response have given up on themselves having a better life, and what they once envisioned. They're so caught up in their little world of "can't do," "don't want change," or "who cares, anyway?" that they miss the boat. I wonder if they've ever even considered helping those they care about, or making their lives better?

All the signs are beckoning but they miss them with their miserable shut-your-eyes-to-the-truth thinking. Misery attracts misery, and the downward spiral continues. They never see the dawn of a beautiful new day, until they wake up and notice what those who are winning are all about—and see how they can transcend their own situation.

Since those first three questions in the opening paragraph of this section can never be answered in present tense, many choose not to become the first in their sphere of influence to do something new. However, history is loaded with countless people who could have accomplished more by doing certain new things. Just listen to the if-only-I-had regretful questions that start with "*What if...?*" only to end in a negative prediction or a woe-is-me afterthought.

Consider these examples:

- *What if* franchising had been declared illegal by the United States Congress?
- *What if* the stock market never goes above 3,000, 6,000, 12,000, 15,000, 20,000?
- *What if* I had invested in land in the 60s, 70s, 80s, 90s, 2000s?

There are many others, some of which may even have affected you. If you regret missing an opportunity, let go of thinking about what you missed and leave the past behind where it belongs. The opportunity *you* need to say yes to that can shape your future could well be right in front of you, complete with the noes! If you thought there wouldn't be any noes associated with the opportunity to move ahead, think again! Remember, getting yes starts when *you* say yes!

Not much good can happen for you unless you're open to it. If you believe nothing works except what you're doing, that's all you can ever hope to attain. Using that line to prove they're not cut out for greater success makes people hide behind the so-called security of their job, happy with it or not. It's simply a false belief. Fortunately, it can be changed.

When an opportunity presents itself, people who accept their lot in life and are used to following the crowd, often feel as if they have no choice but to turn it down. They believe risktakers are destined to lose. Perhaps they've conditioned themselves to focus on negative results. Seldom focusing on the positive, the news media usually creates dramatic headlines out of failures and setbacks. By the time people reach adulthood, it's easier to believe in negatives than positives—noes rather than yeses.

Test it out for yourself. The next time you see someone you haven't seen in a while, notice, first, the clues their appearance offers: are they slogging along looking down, or standing tall, radiating enthusiasm? Sincerely ask how things are going. If they seem excited about life, stop and think about your initial reaction. Are you asking yourself, "What are they hiding?"

Or are they moaning and groaning about the economy, how tough and unfair things are at work, and how life just isn't going their way? Can you relate to that? Have you ever said, "I know what you mean"? Have you ever looked askance at happy, successful people?

What if you could change your life by changing your outlook? *What if* success is made up more of attitude rather than aptitude? *What if* yeses come after noes? *What if* all you had to do was ask "What if...?" to any life-enhancing idea you can think of? What if you make the decision to take the steps required to take full advantage of an idea, and go on your way toward accomplishing your dream or objective?

Many who've been harboring a negative focus and perspective and have never asked themselves about the possibilities for improvement, at first find this hard to believe. Others give it a brief try, only to drop the ball, quitting at the first no. That's the problem—they *tried*. They didn't honestly *do* what they said they were going to do. Doing is the only thing that makes things happen. Trying doesn't work. They didn't stay with it. Their life has been a series of quitting episodes—quitting on themselves, their families, and others. They let a little two-letter word, no, stop them. Imagine that!

Yet there are people all over the world who are living the life they want. They started their journey, often with much less going for them than you or I, essentially with one simple question: What if I really could change my life for the better by not letting no stop me?

Avoid the Anything's-Possible Trap—*Press On!*

Wouldn't it be great to win the lottery? Can you see yourself being more successful?

Have you ever been asked those questions? More importantly, have you ever asked them of yourself? What answers did you come up with? Many people who never seem to move ahead, halfheartedly say, shrugging their shoulders with resignation, "Anything's possible." For them it's just words they've heard before from others who are in the same boat. They passively take whatever comes their way, afraid to face no and gain a better life.

The problem is, that attitude leaves the future strictly to luck—up in the air, as they say. No action is required on their behalf, since they believe it wouldn't do any good anyway. Do you believe whatever good or bad luck comes your way largely determines the life you lead? If so, be of good cheer. If you're not where you want to be, you could be about to change your own luck. Sound good?

> *"Success is connected with action. Successful people keep moving. They make mistakes, but they don't quit."*
> —CONRAD HILTON

Imagine standing at the edge of an enormous field where it is well-known that a rare coin worth $100,000 is out there somewhere. You look at the vast expanse and decide you'd have to be extremely lucky to find *anything* in a field this big, and dismiss the idea of looking for it.

Or perhaps you're a collector who sees the coin as the crowning touch to your collection. You make a grid of the field and focus, one at a time, on small sections, moving onto the next one only after you've completely searched every inch of the one beneath your feet. Your focus is on finding the coin—*no matter what.*

Given a choice, who would you say stands the better chance of success? Who is luck going to favor? No doubt, you can see a marked difference in the attitude that could either stifle or perpetuate success, and how the lack of clarity could negatively affect the outcome. If so, perhaps you need to change your thinking about how taking consistent action can stack the odds in your favor.

If you live life noncommittally, the waves of change and other's agendas dash you as they will. It's as if you're a fragile tree in the wind, breaking when the turbulence of change overpowers you. Many feel like they're on an endless treadmill. But rather than continuing with the grind, they need to focus on what they really want.

Visualize your objective clearly and believe "this is doable as long as I keep going." Refuse the idea that success is luck or a mere chance happening. See yourself never giving up. Seek out tools and people who can help you achieve your goal.

You no longer allow the things that used to distract you get in your way. You no longer make excuses either. As you buy into yes and your ability to achieve it, your determination and motivation increase. When you get a no, or when things don't go exactly according to plan, you learn, adjust, and go at it again, rather than surrendering in defeat. You see far too many who let no snatch their dream, and you're committed to not letting no determine your future. You have one life to live and you're going to live it—with vigor and enthusiasm. No doesn't stop you anymore, and you're certain you'll grow into attracting the yeses that shape your future.

You're committed to always going the extra mile—no matter what it takes—rather than doing the bare minimum. You've bought into your potential for yes, rather than selling out to no. That simple change can take you from making a living, to living a life of more adventure and accomplishment.

"Failure is the opportunity to begin again more intelligently."

—HENRY FORD

2

Use No to Leverage Your Way to Yes

hen I was working to get my first book published, over 100 publishers said no before I was offered a contract. That's not counting those who didn't even have the courtesy to respond! One of the most frequent questions I've been asked is, "John, how could you keep going in spite of all the noes?"

I'd love to give you a profound answer that would change your life. But all I can say is that I always believed yes was just around the corner. I never realized how many publishers had said no until I counted all the rejection letters—after I signed that first contract! I learned that noes really don't matter! It was that one yes that determined my future.

My goal was to be published. I needed only one publisher who believed enough in my manuscript to say yes. That's the only answer that mattered to me. And since that was the one answer I wanted, I kept going until I got it. As it turned out, though, it wasn't for the manuscript I had submitted. Believe it or not, they actually rejected it! But after reviewing it, they asked if I'd be interested in writing a book on rejection. So my first book, *Reject Me—I love It!* was born out of no! I was able to turn a no into a yes by following the guidance of the publisher, turning rejection into a new direction! Your reading this book, my ninth now, is proof enough that the method I used was effective, and can be applied to other endeavors.

Another facet of the story is that it took over two years to be told no 100 times. I sent out a proposal every week whether I had received an answer from a publisher or not. When I got a no, I simply put it in a folder. It didn't stop me from sending an improved proposal to the next publisher.

Still, 100 noes does seem like an awful lot, doesn't it? But it all depends on your perspective. If I had wasted time counting noes, dwelling on and being discouraged by each one, I could have easily become overwhelmed and quit. I could have let doubt erode my confidence as an author, preventing me from making the improvements needed for a quality product.

Fortunately, I never thought of doing that. I was so focused on seeing my name on the cover of a book that, if necessary, I would still be mailing proposals today to find a publisher. I focused on getting one yes, and kept going until I got it.

I can't say how many times you'll hear no while pursuing your objective. I can't tell you how long it'll take either. But I can tell you this. You'll always have a chance of reaching yes as long as you don't allow no to determine your future.

It's Not Time—*It's Yes That Matters Most!*

While it took two years of noes before I got my first yes, that's no indication of how long it will take you to get a yes to what you're doing. In achieving success, time is seldom the issue—it'll take whatever time it takes for you to do it. That doesn't mean you should drag your feet either. Persist until you get the job done. When you do, keep going and set an even bigger goal, while repeating the process!

Maybe your success will occur after only one no, ten noes, a hundred noes, or maybe even a thousand noes. When you're committed to yes it just doesn't matter. The time it takes to hear each answer is not carved in stone either. Nor is it true that it will take less time to hear 10 noes than it will to hear 1,000. When you step up the pace of sharing or doing something, though, things can go more quickly—as long as you learn from mistakes made along the way.

Each answer is merely a step in a predetermined direction. Choose a path with a destination firmly in mind. There's no specific time limit on how long it takes to get there. Accomplishment is based on taking steps—putting one foot in front of the other, making one call after the other, or doing whatever else is needed—not time.

> "I haven't failed. I've found 10,000 ways that don't work."
> —BENJAMIN FRANKLIN

My goal in getting a book published was 100 noes away from the moment I got the first yes. It took 100 noes for me to get where I wanted to be. That was *my* journey. That's just what it took for me to get a yes, based on the way I approached the goal. It's an historical fact. However, nothing said it had to take two years. That was *my* choice.

I could have sent out two letters a week and probably reached my objective within a year. But *what if*—there's that question again—I had sent out one letter a day? It's entirely possible I would have reached my goal in only 100 days. What if I had sent out one letter an hour? Is it possible the process would have been dramatically speeded up? Yes!

How soon you get a yes is often determined by the time you spend on a given no. If you dwell on each no, maybe feeling sorry for yourself as you commiserate with others at length about it, risking another no becomes more difficult. This is exactly why some people give up on their dreams and goals. They focus on the noes and let them take control and determine their future. Rather than understanding the importance of no for their growth on the journey to yes, they give up on their quest. Remember, no is the only way to yes!

It's Not Really *"Just a Numbers Game"*

In many sales training programs people are taught that the more noes they get, the closer they are to making a sale. They're told the odds increase in their favor after each no. It sounds as if it's simply a matter of luck as to who says yes. The impression is that all you need to do is keep asking.

While there's a certain amount of truth to that, you can only *hope* to get yes if you don't learn from the noes. Take more responsibility for handling and learning from the responses you receive. This keeps you on the cutting edge of growth. Look at ways to improve your resilience, compassion, understanding, and expertise in working with others. Increase your knowledge, your presentation, and other skills and attitudes. Incorporate them into whatever you're doing.

Consider the 100 noes I went through to get published. According to some, that meant the odds finally caught up with me, rewarding my persistence. But I don't believe that for a minute. If that were true, I could have signed a contract sooner if I had only written to the publisher who said yes sooner. But there's more to it than that!

What ultimately led to my first contract was a *combination* of persistence and adjustments. I made improvements, then submitted the adjusted proposal to the next publisher. In essence, I fine-tuned, grew, and got better. It's a lifelong process and part of the adventure of living a great life!

The results will speak for themselves. Stick to your aspirations and constantly strive to achieve them. Make adjustments along the way as needed to shorten the trip. Had I continued sending out my original proposal, I would, no doubt, still be spending time and money on paper and postage, my dream far off in the distance.

Improving your relationships, methods, skills, services, ideas, and offerings will help give you more of an edge—over anybody or anything that can compete with you—and it'll keep you growing. Embrace the wisdom of those leading the way. Follow their guidance and your ability to attract more yeses into your life will improve.

No Means *You Need to Grow!*

Think about the difference between yes and no in terms of a job. A yes from the boss could equate to a raise, whereas no might mean maintaining the status quo or even losing the job.

Consider the difference between yes and no in building a business. Every day, put in as much time and effort as possible. Growth comes from learning and developing what's being done to meet the needs of the people being served. Reading, evaluating, and taking advantage of the resources available in support of achieving yes are all part of the leveraging process.

Yes and no are tremendous teachers. When someone says yes, that means you got it right enough for that person and that situation. But remember, there's always room to grow. It also means you may well hear yes again when you have a similar kind of person in the same type of situation. Regardless of the outcome, though, keep plugging and never give up. If those who said no did so because your presentation was weak or faulty, something in *you* needs to change. Keep growing to where you can approach them more effectively.

Get involved in continuing education, growing your skills, your knowledge base, and attitude. No is a signal to learn, teaching you how to get yes more easily. No means you need to grow! You may say, "But timing on their part was the concern." Agreed, timing plays a part in every endeavor. This means you need to continue extending the hand of friendship, even if you're disappointed in their response and feel rejected. You may need to grow in compassion and patience to do that— have a tough skin but a tender heart. You could even revisit a previous no and possibly see it turn into a yes! Why? You cared enough and grew in the interim, while their situation also may have changed.

Experience noes and you'll grow by blasting through the obstacles. This will help you reduce the noes, maximizing your ability to head off the most common reasons for being told no—before they become issues! Make a study of dealing with objections, applying what insights you gain as you go. Be daring and have fun with this! Remember, you're not alone. That's just how it works.

Again, I'm not suggesting you expect to be told no. Always go for yes, using no as a sign to press on and grow. By the same token, when someone says yes, don't stop then either. It's time to deliver. You've found a need, now fill it. Give them your best while continuing to grow.

> *"Most notable winners encountered heartbreaking obstacles before they triumphed. They win because they refused to become discouraged by their defeats."*
>
> —B.C. FORBES

When someone says no it's a sign for you to explore how to minimize getting a no in the future. Discover how to better deliver your presentation so you can avoid certain noes from ever coming up. Always be open to the possibility of sharing ideas and asking questions that could cause them to open their minds and accept what you're offering. Change is inevitable in life and in dealing with others. The great news is you can be a positive change agent! Stretch and be proactive while helping and encouraging others to do the same, especially in handling noes.

If you're not willing to risk getting a no, there's no way someone can ever accept you or your offering. To achieve yes, you need to risk hearing no! You need to overcome your own objections and excuses, your own noes, before you'll be able to assist others in overcoming theirs.

Tell *Yourself* No When Necessary—*Be Self-Disciplined*

If you want to be more successful, say no to TV. Say no to playing on the Internet. Say no to your kids if they want things you can't afford or you don't think they should have. Say no to doing things or going places that take you off track from your objective. Say no to yourself, as appropriate.

Discipline yourself to say no to whatever is hindering you from getting where you're going, but say a big YES to the life you really want. It's not always easy, but it's essential if you're serious about making it a reality. Do what's truly best for you and your family. Anyone left in the wake of those changes will be taken care of. Your investment in yourself will prove best for them in the long-run as well. They'll see.

"There is no limit to what can be accomplished if it doesn't matter who gets the credit."

—RALPH WALDO EMERSON

3

It's Not About You!

So what does the world owe you for your efforts? As a reward for persistence and commitment to my dream, I finally felt it was time to bask in the spotlight. I believed the reasons for my success were focus and hard work. The results were what I thought I had rightfully earned.

It was my first opportunity to be the keynote speaker at a large convention. I had heard about how well the lead-off presenter was treated, and thought this was my reward for the years of effort I had put forth. The organization used my books and asked me to speak to their people about what it took to achieve success. I painstakingly prepared every word.

The program went well, as the audience stood shouting in appreciation. All I could think of as I walked off stage was, "This was the reason I had worked so hard." This was my reward for everything I had sacrificed and done without. I thought I knew why I should continue writing and speaking—for recognition.

I was taken to a table outside the convention hall and asked to sign books. A mob of people were saying hello, asking for autographs. I was in my glory. All I could think about was how this must be what being successful is all about.

After a while, I noticed the next program was about to begin. All the attendees were entitled to hear from every speaker, so I announced I would shut down the table until after the next presentation was over. I assured them I would be back when they came out.

As they departed, I realized I hadn't been off my feet in quite a while. I slumped into a chair near the table and put my head down to take a breather. Suddenly, I noticed a shadow looming over me and lifted my head. There he stood. As I looked at him dressed in a shirt that was too large, a jacket that had seen better days, and a tie shiny from wear, I wanted to escape. The redness in his eyes caused me to think the worst. However, nothing could have been further from the truth.

He had been crying since my talk and waited until everyone had gone into the auditorium before he came over to see me. Nervous and teary-eyed, he explained, "I've never attended any of these events because I couldn't afford them. But this one I just couldn't afford to miss." He was clutching a well-worn copy of *Reject Me—I Love It!*

"I've come to meet you," he said, lips quivering. "Someone gave me this book at a time when I was thinking of cashing it all in." I was hoping he was talking about something else but knew he wasn't. "There wasn't much going on in my life to make me want to hang around. Then I read this." He held the book up, his hand shaking in front of my face. "I came here this weekend to say thank you for writing this for me."

He turned and hurriedly walked back into the auditorium before I could say anything near resembling a response. As the door closed behind him, I might have muttered a weak thank you. I was shaking all over. As I once again collapsed into the chair, my head began to spin. All the reasons I had for doing what I do were wrong. I wasn't speaking for the audience. I wasn't successful because of me. I was where I was, doing what I do—*for him!*

That was many years ago. But writing about it makes me certain I'll never forget why I do what I do. As a result, I close every presentation with this message:

> I don't claim to have all the answers. For many of you I may have no answer at all. But for one of you I may have *the* answer that makes a difference in your life. If you're here searching, reaching, I hope I've helped. You're the reason I came. All I ask in return is that you find someone else who could use an answer and give it to them unconditionally.

Negative Motivation—*How Dare You Keep It from Them?*

Did you ever get nervous about something? Have you ever thought about not doing something because of how it might be perceived? Have you ever put something off for no apparent reason? Perhaps you need a bit of negative motivation to get going in the right direction.

> *"Nothing, not all the armies in the world, can stop an idea whose time has come."*
>
> —VICTOR HUGO

When I work with writers at a conference or seminar, I'm amazed at how many of them haven't begun writing their books yet. Asking why, I'm given a multitude of reasons or, more accurately, excuses. They invariably say they can't find the time, never develop the proper frame of mind, or simply have writer's block. Since most of them come for assistance in writing self-help or inspirational material, I ask them a series of questions to give them a boost in getting going.

First I ask, "Do you believe in your concept?" Then I ask, "Do you feel your book will help others make positive changes in their lives?" Once they say yes, I hit them with a negative motivational question, demanding, "Since you all agree that your book is going to change lives, how dare you keep it from them?" This makes them realize that each day they delay does more than simply put off the completion of their book. All of a sudden, they consider the possible harm others will endure if they don't shift some priorities and make the time to get it done. The idea is to jolt them into transforming their indecision and inaction into doing what's theirs to do—take action.

What would happen if you followed that practice in facing tough decisions? When you broaden your vision, you begin to see more of those who will be affected by your decisions. This can be a big benefit when the decision you have to make is one that causes fear and anxiety. When you understand how doing the right thing could help create what's best for you and others, making the decision isn't quite so difficult. When you care enough about others who stand to benefit, it's easier to make the right choice and take action on it, not letting non-believers stop you.

Do You Focus with a Microscope or a Telescope?

Once you determine your path for success, stay focused. Dwelling on obstacles and challenges, or giving in to the temptation to stray from your chosen path, only cause you to lose focus on the objective. You begin falling back into old habits that don't serve you or others, making it more difficult to stay on track. You get what you focus on—good, bad, or indifferent. It's an irrefutable law!

Focusing with a microscope, when done from an optimistic perspective, takes you to your goal in minute detail. You start realizing what it will be like once you accomplish what you've set out to do. You begin owning your goal and start feeling what it would be like to miss it, making you all the more determined in the quest.

In creating that level of detail, you're able to see your own hidden strengths. You may discover that you already have the tools and the opportunity to reach your destination.

Focusing with a telescope brings things in the distance closer, enabling you to see beyond what you're normally capable of seeing. It brings into view what may seem a long way off. It's also how to best look at people.

Unlike the microscope, which looks at the smallest detail or fault, the telescope allows you to look beyond what's right in front of you, out past the horizon. When you look at people through a telescope, you see their true potential. You look beyond their current state or status, and can focus on what they can become.

With microscopic focus, you can get bogged down with others' minor faults and habits. This kind of focus is better suited to tasks where detail can prove important. But for individuals, focusing on little faults only magnifies them in your eyes. This may lead you to making detrimental decisions in dealing with them, causing you to harbor resentment and unforgiveness. How would you feel if someone put their emphasis only on your less-developed points and failed to recognize the good you have to offer? Might they be doing you an injustice? Definitely!

When you see people in light of their potential—the bigger picture—you'll find it easier to maintain your patience in working with them. You see the outcome and the benefit of their reaching their highest level of performance. You're far less likely to allow them to get down on themselves or fall by the wayside. Remember how certain people have patiently supported you over the years? We all need to receive and give the gift of patience every day!

You need both microscopic and telescopic focus to attain your objective. Both are invaluable tools and, when properly used, can accelerate reaching your destination in a manner that brings others along as well.

Using the *microscope* on your *mission* and the *telescope* to *teach* is critical to long-lasting success. It's not about you or me. It's about supporting others in realizing the potential they have inside, while zeroing in on and making the changes needed to achieve the goal. This is the most direct way to achieve greater success.

"A pessimist sees the difficulty in every opportunity; the optimist sees the opportunity in every difficulty."

—L.P. JACKS

4

Look at Believing in the Possibilities of Yes

There are those who moan and groan their way through life, taking whatever comes along, playing the victim role to the max, saying no to a better life. When asked about planning for the future they often say, "Since there are no guarantees, I'll just live for today." But are they living a wonderful life or just surviving?

Contrary to popular thinking, believe in guarantees! If you do nothing to change your thinking and your future, you actually predict it. You virtually guarantee it will be filled with more of your past and present. You'll only get more noes along the way. If you're not preparing for the future—making each second, minute, hour, and day count—you don't have much of one to look forward to.

There are always nuances and variations in other people and their behaviors that can affect your outcome—at least temporarily. But if you allow these events to throw you off track permanently, you're making a big mistake. The future is inevitable; it's going to happen one way or another. But you can be a catalyst for positive change when you follow your own path, even if it requires you to go against the tide. The waves you make may be rough—change causes that and rocks the boat. But you can handle it!

How you'll be treated in the future has yet to be determined. But if you acquiesce and simply let it happen, it will unfold in whatever direction the wind blows. The choice is yours.

Taking action doesn't mean you'll always achieve your objective exactly the way you want. But it sets you in motion on the path of progress—it gets you rolling. Keenly focus on where you want to go and you'll be more tuned in to doing whatever it takes along the way. You'll address issues in a firm yet friendly way, adapt to change, and create success habits. Correct your course as needed, and keep pushing through the challenges until you're victorious.

Simply taking action doesn't necessarily mean you'll arrive at your chosen destination either. You need to take the *right* actions—the ones that will get you where you're going as quickly and efficiently as possible. Keep your eyes on the objective, periodically looking in your side and rear view mirrors. Focus on where you're going while navigating around the potholes.

If you take your eyes off the course, you can't stay on the path. If you lose sight of where you want to go, it'll be impossible to get there.

You Don't Have to Get Lost—*Road Maps Are Available*

You don't always have to start from scratch. While experience is the best teacher, there's nothing written saying it has to all be yours! Save yourself a lot of grief and aggravation by following the path and guidance of others who are where you want to be.

Early on in high school, when my son decided he wanted to get a scholarship and pitch at the college level, I helped him with his planning. I suggested he find some successful ballplayers, learn what they did to improve, then work harder than anyone else. He found a few players who were having the kind of success he wanted and began following their example. As of this writing, he's enjoying college on a baseball scholarship and is focused on playing professionally. He believes he can do it—*and so do I!*

So where do you want to be? Is there someone you admire who's already there, or at least further along than you are? That's someone you might want to emulate. Perhaps you can even get close enough to that person to ask if they would be your coach or mentor. They could help you avoid mistakes similar to ones they've already made, while encouraging you to keep going.

> *"Our chief want in life is somebody who will make us do what we can."*
>
> —RALPH WALDO EMERSON

Coaches and mentors may not be perfect, but they're experienced and can help you succeed. They can't help you avoid every mistake, but they can encourage you to stay the course. If you get off track, they can help you get back on and stay focused better than you could on your own. They'll guide you in overcoming obstacles, while cheering you on. They're also people you can be accountable to; something we all need.

Belief Creates Vision—*Opening the Door to Yes*

We've all heard the expression: "I'll believe it when I see it." While seeing something is proof it exists, not seeing it doesn't prove it doesn't!

Ever hear the expression, "You'll see it when you believe it"? Before any new accomplishment worthy of mention, there's first bold belief then decided determination. Without that, it would be difficult to maintain the optimistic, open-minded attitude that asks, "What are the possibilities for yes?" Believing with gumption is like encouraging yourself, cheering yourself on. When you believe with conviction that you can do something—that you can get a yes—you can! Keep your belief strong, so you're not tempted to make an excuse or otherwise justify giving up, which only leads to regret.

Belief fuels drive. It keeps us going when others try to hold us back. When people doubt you or your potential, use it as a catalyst to move on—to show them. It's an essential ingredient for maintaining commitment. It keeps you from even considering the noes of others, while directing you to keep your eyes riveted on your destination.

Sight prevents you from blindly tripping over the obstacles in front of you, while vision enables you to see the yeses in overcoming them. Strong belief creates a strong vision. As your belief in yourself and the process of achieving expands and intensifies, your vision of the yeses life has in store for you becomes clearer. Steadily focusing on the vision with dogged determination propels you into appropriate action.

You Can See Only What You *Believe*

None of us have approached our maximum potential as each of us has certain self- or other-imposed limits, reflecting the beliefs we've adopted over the years. But we don't have to stay stuck with them. We can raise the ceiling and surprise both ourselves and others with what we can really do. It all depends on our belief.

> *"One person with a belief is equal to a force of ninety-nine who have only interest."*
>
> —JOHN STUART MILL

While I don't foresee most reaching or even getting close to any limits, those who work to excel beyond the experiences and activities of an ordinary life will test and stretch beyond the limits. In my case, I've never invented anything, nor have I developed a cure for any disease. I've never even had any thoughts about doing things in those areas. Although these would be worthy accomplishments, my lack of desire to do so has prevented me from moving in those directions.

There just isn't enough time to do everything we admire others for doing. That's okay. We simply need to pursue our *own* path. Don't follow the herd, like most. Some of them are only going to slaughter—living lives of disappointment, regret, and not-so-quiet desperation.

What really needs attention are the thoughts and desires you *do* have about what you want your life experience to be. That's what ignites your enthusiasm. You have the capacity to pursue anything you can passionately imagine. Push on the edge of whatever limits you or others may be imposing on you. This will make the foundational difference in what you accomplish.

Your mind is incredible. No idea that fires your enthusiasm can come into it that you don't have the ability or potential ability to make happen. Yet far too many people discount their lives by just taking things as they come. They're continuously frustrated—lacking fulfillment and true happiness. Take some time to think about what excites you, then go for it.

We all have an enormous potential which we can take advantage of, but only when we're truly open to the possibilities. The yeses can increase dramatically when you believe in yourself, home in on what you want, and let your inspired mind help you in developing the right thought pattern to guide you.

Your mind will point you to people who can help, as well as create ideas that can develop into yeses to overcome whatever noes you might encounter along the way. Believe and trust in yourself that you *do* have the capacity to further develop from the seeds of your thought. All success begins in the mind. You cannot have a victory in reality until you have victory in the mind. Believe in the possibilities of yes!

"Sometimes it is not enough to do your best; you have to do what's required."

—Winston Churchill

5

Dare to Keep Getting *Better* than Your Best!

How are you doing? What was your response? Might it have been something like, "Oh, I'm hangin' in there"? Beware. Too many people are just getting by, doing okay, maintaining their so-so position by avoiding the possibility of no.

With change constantly going on around us, it's generally impossible to get anywhere just being what we've always been. Try to hold on to "your spot," and the world passes you by. Not because you necessarily did anything wrong, mind you. But as things change, that spot you worked to get to is still just a spot, and it's probably getting a bit old. Others have moved beyond it as they learned and grew, perhaps without thinking about it. It was just the natural thing to do—*move on rather than hold on.* "Used to died," a friend's mother observed.

Still not convinced? Let's put it into a frame of reference that's easy to see—income.

When you landed your first job and learned what you'd be getting paid, what did you think? For me, it was after I got out of the military and began selling cars at a local dealership. The people I worked for diligently helped me work more effectively with each customer, according to their needs, wants, and ability to pay. I worked hard, followed their lead, and did very well. I was earning what I thought was big money.

Newly married, we were living with my mother-in-law until we got ourselves established. We had no bills to speak of so my take-home pay was available to spend. That was over 25 years ago. I wouldn't want to imagine going back to earning that same "big" money today. Why not? What changed?

Two kids, one in college, the other in private school. Property taxes, insurance, dentists, and such. You get the picture. Had my income not progressed beyond ordinary raises and cost of living increases, it would have been nearly impossible, financially, to raise a family. It would have stressed us out with debt. Had my skills and experience stagnated, my income couldn't have reached the levels needed for the life I wanted to live.

I soon realized that to get paid more I had to get more yeses and make decisions that affected more people. How many people are you affecting? Are you paid at the level where you can do what you want when you want?

Don't misunderstand; if you love your career and financial status, that's great. If you've been fortunate enough to find something you enjoy doing for a living that pays well, wonderful. But what if your skills don't keep pace with the progress you'd like to make? What if you're in a lurch or approaching one? You may find yourself on the outside looking in or, at best, looking up from the lower levels as others pass you by.

Evaluate Your Past Efforts—*and Harvest More Yeses*

Hopefully you've enjoyed and gleaned something from what you've read so far. I've worked diligently to improve my writing over the years, using my experience and that of other writers, my editors and publishers, and other people I respect. I trust you'll learn something from *Yes!* that propels you to heights unimagined.

I was satisfied with the way my earlier books had developed. But if I hadn't been continuously striving, challenging myself to grow and become *better* than my best, many who have read those books would feel I have nothing more to offer. However, I didn't just expand and refine my skills because I kept writing; quite the opposite. I kept writing because I had more to share having grown through various challenges—more noes and failings—life continued to throw my way.

You, too, can maximize your yes rate by challenging yourself, continuously growing, getting better with practice. But to truly impact your ability to get more yeses, you need to evaluate what you've done in the past. Even if you've become a smashing success in what you've focused on in the past, be humble in seeking the help of others in doing new things. Past successes in getting yes don't necessarily translate into getting instant yeses at something new.

> *"Good is not good where better is expected."*
> —THOMAS FULLER

The old saying "It's not what you say, but how you say it" really applies here. Simply asking yourself, "Could I have done better?" may not do the trick. You may reflect on your efforts and let your ego get in the way of admitting you could have aced it if you had *really* applied yourself. Avoid second-guessing your work. First, acknowledge that, based on what you knew and when you knew it, you put out whatever level of effort you did to create the outcome you got.

Now give yourself another chance to improve. Ask yourself *the* question:

"If there's one thing I could have done to improve on what I've already done, what would it be?" If necessary, wait a while for the answer. Once you have it, armed with new insight, you can increase your ability to harvest yeses. The improvement could be applied to all areas of your life, making a major difference. Your next effort will reflect a new level of thinking, including the benefits of everything you've experienced up to that point, plus the one improvement you just thought of. It all adds to forward motion.

Past Noes and Failures *Do Not Determine Your Future*

As you improve, let go of any tendency you might have to get hung up on the past. Sometimes we can let a no or should-have-done thought cloud what we have really accomplished. Recall your past yeses and victories, and how far you've come in whatever areas you've made strides. You did well before and you can do well again. Whatever foibles you've had since then, they need not ruin your attitude toward the good you've done in the past.

Beating yourself up over past noes and failures is fruitless and saps your energy. Let them stay back there in the past where they belong! We've all made our share of mistakes; don't let outside appearances fool you. Past noes and failures do not determine your future…unless you let them!

> *"The majority of people meet with failure because of their lack of persistence in creating new [approaches] to take the place of those that fail."*
>
> —NAPOLEON HILL

Think about when you were in school. Imagine a test with 100 questions. You studied and were prepared. When you got the test back you found you had only one wrong answer. Great. But even though you were correct 99 times out of a 100, you decide to review how you did. You ask yourself, "What one thing could I have done to improve my performance?"

The obvious answer is you could have responded to that one question correctly! It's the only thing you could've done better. But, does the fact that you found something to improve upon in any way diminish your getting a ninety-nine? Absolutely not! Is there any point in becoming discouraged or depressed over the fact that you could have done better? No! Just learn from it and move on.

Evaluate what you could have done better simply to help yourself from now on—not to beat yourself up over a past you can't change. Use your energy in a positive, moving-forward manner.

Have You Ever Said, *"But I Did My Best"?*

"But I did my best." Ever say that? We all have, for one reason or another, with various motives, not thinking much about it. Part of the challenge is that best is usually considered the maximum possible. But best is really a pronouncement of the end of the line! Best is as good as it gets. While doing *the* best is a positive thing, doing *your* best may not be! You need to do what is *required!*

What if you're not yet where you want to be? How can you expect to achieve greater things while telling yourself you did your best? What if you've said that simply to mask a less-than-hearty effort?

Before you argue that this is an exercise in semantics, let's review the power of thought and its translation into action. Since you're a believer in achieving worthy aspirations, it would be natural to assume that doing your best will get you there. But, by definition, your best is all you can possibly do—you've reached the extent of your capabilities.

Yes, giving it 100 percent is critical to achieving success. However, 100 percent is not necessarily your ultimate best effort. It just means you gave everything you had to accomplish what you did—at that particular time, at that level of awareness, and at that stage of your personal development. If you've reached your objective, it's more likely you gave it 100 percent. But maybe you didn't. It might just have been a relatively easy goal for you to achieve. If you set your goal too low, frankly, it was no great accomplishment. But, one way or the other, if you didn't accomplish it, take some deep breaths, relax, regroup, and give it all you've got.

Whatever you do, let go of ever again saying you did your best. Saying "But I did my best," triggers a harmful change in your thought process for achieving that objective. Instead of prompting resourcefulness about how to get there, you start rationalizing, grabbing for reasons (excuses!) as to why you didn't get there! Rather than mustering up your courage and determination in facing the possibility of no and failing, falling short of your target date, again, you may flippantly change objectives, opting for the safe-but-sorry route. You may figure that's a lot of work you no longer have to do. You may give up on the valued objective you had and replace it with the emptiness of repeated regret.

Instead of excusing yourself from accomplishing your goal by resignedly saying, "But I did my best," take a moment and tell yourself what is needed to do *better*. When you do, two things will happen.

First, you're telling yourself that the goal is still possible and you're acknowledging the need to keep going and growing until you reach it. Then your mind begins coming up with solutions to help you get closer to what you're aiming for—*yes!* Remember, the answer to how is yes!

Challenging yourself to constantly look for and implement ways of becoming better will benefit not only you but others as well. They'll be more inclined to turn to you, knowing you're on the grow and applying the most effective ways to accomplish tasks, as well as support them.

If you take your eyes off where you want to be, retreat, and become satisfied with where you are, the best settles in for a long, progress-thwarting stay. As long as you're consistently looking for better and enthusiastically implementing it, there will always be stimulating goals to set and yeses to achieve.

> *"Desire is the key to motivation, but it's the determination and commitment to an unrelenting pursuit of your goal—a commitment to excellence—that will enable you to attain the success you seek."*
>
> —MARIO ANDRETTI

The problem with best is that it's final. There's nothing more! Once you've done your best, it's game over. It's far more powerful and exciting to engage yourself in doing *better*. Believe you can do better with each effort, and you'll increase the probability of yes. Until you do, though, the light of hope is always on. As long as there's room for improvement, and there generally is, you can take the appropriate steps and gain momentum, moving closer to where you want to be.

If you did what was required, great. Consider it your best, but only for that objective. If you didn't do what was required, learn how you can fine-tune to achieve your next goal. Through it all, though, be sure to notice the gains you've been making. Some search their entire lives for a certain success only to discover they've been experiencing it incrementally all along; they just didn't recognize it. Enjoy the fruits of continuous accomplishment. It helps provide perspective and balance, reinforcing the idea that sufficient belief, followed by sustained effort, can lead to desired results.

Complacency is the enemy of progress. Far too many people have already proved that if you stay the same, you'll actually fall behind. Life-long growth, becoming better than your best, is essential for achieving yes. Persist in paying the price that leads to yes. The satisfaction resulting from pursuing your path is immeasurable.

"If you want one year of prosperity; grow grain;
If you want ten years of prosperity; grow trees;
If you want 100 years of prosperity; grow people."
—CHINESE PROVERB

6

Investing in Your Own Growth Takes Time but Offers You the Greatest Return

hat would you think of someone who put $10,000 in the bank one day and withdrew it the next, just to stuff it in a bag in a closet? What would you say to them if they began complaining about a lack of earnings?

Obviously, money doesn't grow the instant it's invested. In fact, there are often fees associated with opening and maintaining the investment. Growth depends on how much you invest, where you invest it, the rate of return, and how long you let it work for you. So why do people fall into the instant-gratification trap when it comes to improving their lives? Why don't they understand that the investment they make in their own personal growth requires time and energy to yield fruit? Be patient while you grow. Give yourself time to succeed.

For example, achieving and maintaining a healthy weight used to require long-term thinking and habit changes. It still does! While advertisers would have you believe all it takes is a pill or a quick-fix, flash-in-the-pan diet, neither delivers. Learning a language used to be about attending classes, studying, and practicing. Now it's supposedly about listening to CDs while on a plane to that country. I don't think so.

Improving your own performance once required a commitment to make changes and grow through the noes over a period of time. It still does! Everyone wants a book, CD, or another casual agent to solve their problems for them today, right now. But it just doesn't work that way! These things can help, but unless we apply what we've learned, they are just diversions. Being an information junkie doesn't get the job done.

It's like going to the gym on Thursday, expecting to have the body you want on Friday—then being angry when it doesn't happen. Some people try to shift responsibility, blaming everyone and everything for their lack of results. They never think of looking in the proverbial mirror at the one person who can make all the difference—themselves! They don't get it that the one who has the dream or aspiration needs to take the lead in getting it done. Who else is going to do it? Who else suffers most if it isn't done? Who else says, "Maybe I could have...," with a woeful-looking face?

Life improvement takes time, so make it part of your everyday activities. Keep learning and doing things, over and over again, fine-tuning as you go, until you achieve what you've set out to do. Learning and implementing then become unconscious, a part of your very being—a habit pattern for success.

Generating a Return on Your Investment in You

There has to be a reason, a reward for investing in yourself. Whether it's more time with your loved ones, more money, or something else, there must be a big enough payoff. Otherwise, why bother? That's why many investments don't pay off. People often begin randomly investing without clearly defining their objectives, let alone getting proper guidance.

Without a desired outcome, including progress indicators to let you know how you're doing, would you know you've accomplished your goal or achieved success? How well have you identified a payoff that's worth all the effort? Will that thrust you into action? These questions are critical if you expect to have a chance at greater success. Having a definite target will prevent you from shooting in the dark, missing the mark.

Imagine changing your eating and exercising habits without a target weight in mind. How unhealthy would it be to continue going below the weight where you look and feel great? Not to worry. Most people quit well before they reach the danger zone. But they quit for the same basic reason—they didn't solidly determine where they wanted to go. Their desire wasn't strong enough to go and grow through the noes until they got there. They failed to maintain their new success pattern until it became habitual. They guessed at where they wanted to go.

Most of the time, of course, that guess is wrong, with reality most evident right around the time things get difficult! As with a weight reduction program, especially if the target is a dramatic plummet, the initial weight comes off quickly. Then, as our body acclimates, the weight loss slows down. This is when many quit. If they clearly had a grip on the target, a no-nonsense attitude about it, perhaps they'd keep going with some encouragement.

You've got to have a firm handle on the payoff, *before* you invest your time and energy. Once there's a strong enough value put on the target, something you *really* want, it becomes easier to get and stay excited and press on when the noes come and the going gets tough.

> *"If you don't invest very much, then defeat doesn't hurt very much and winning is not very exciting."*
> —DICK VERMEIL

When deciding on the payoff or the prize you're aiming toward, make it as substantial a gain as possible. This will spur you on. As with any investment, there will be ups and downs over time—it's part of the human condition—the ebb and flow of the achievement cycle. To keep going, believe in a high return; otherwise, every little setback could spell the end and the all-too-common "why bother?" But not bothering has led to countless humdrum existences. Just look around. It makes me shudder just thinking about it. How about you?

Stay the Course—*Yes Comes Only to Those Who Persist*

Not every investment grows as we might like. Even the best planning and execution won't guarantee a good return. While strategizing and focused effort can go a long way in preventing losses, there are things beyond our control that can affect the outcome.

When challenges, i.e., noes, crop up, step back. Survey the field to see where slip-ups occurred and start again—with renewed focus and enthusiasm. Remember, you're going for yes. Keep your goal in focus to bolster and sustain your determination, setting it until it's all achieved.

When your efforts aren't generating the yeses you want, improve your attitude, approach, or action. Take a critical look and see what works and what doesn't. Ask, "How can I make this work better?"

Take an honest look at what you've done so far in life. Have you given maximum effort to what's most important to you? If so, great. Stretch, give it more, and keep going. There's always room for improvement. Remember, by persistence, the snail made it to the Ark!

"Paralyze resistance with persistence."
—WOODY HAGER

If you're holding back, is there something or someone creating an obstacle you don't think you can overcome? What is it? How can you change your thinking and, therefore, your results? Is there another way to do the same thing? How have you responded or reacted to this obstacle? Are you letting it bowl you over? Are you moving forward or procrastinating? Success is in *you*, not in someone else, not in something else, and not in someplace else. Bloom where you're planted! Once people know you're serious about your objective, they might even say to themselves, "There must be something to this. Maybe I should follow their lead."

The other reason for looking at what you've done so far is the energy boost that comes from knowing what you did right. Revel in the small victories on the path to the big one. When you see that out of eight steps, for example, you did six as well as they could have been done, you'll be encouraged. You need to improve in only two areas. Or you may find that everything you've planned was correct, but your effort or thoroughness just wasn't what it could have been.

Have you ever recoiled when you got a no because you didn't counter it with an appropriate question—which could have yielded a yes? Great! That's an exciting discovery because you've been reinforced on what to do the next time. Just put more effort into its execution.

Enjoy the Journey

You've planned, worked, overcome, and, most importantly, never quit—no matter how many noes you've encountered. Now what? That depends on the purpose of achieving your objective. Unfortunately, though, far too many people fail to do the one thing they're entitled to once they've hit the mark, and it's a real danger to hitting their next objective and long-term success. They fail to enjoy the journey, the incremental successes, as they go along.

Failing to take a deep breath, not acknowledging you've accomplished something along the way, diminishes your sense of satisfaction about what you've accomplished. It takes away from all you've done, and can lead to less satisfaction with future tasks. A thankful attitude of gratitude for all the help you may have received is key too. We all need to be generous in our appreciation; a grateful heart is an asset beyond measure and leads to greater relationships.

Let's compare two scenarios of how you'd feel after you accomplish something, if you...

- Start planning the next task without taking the time to refresh and encourage yourself. You plow right into it, not taking stock of what really worked, while feeling ungrateful toward yourself and others.

- Enjoy the fact that you've made it to this point—refreshing and encouraging yourself to take on the next task. You know that with the same persistence and growth, you can do whatever else you set your mind to, as long as you apply yourself. You gain confidence by seeing what you've just accomplished, while identifying the things you'll do better next time. You show appreciation for the help others gave you along they way.

Which of these outcomes do you intend to create? The point is, enjoy the present and the rewards you've earned so far, while forging ahead until you accomplish your objective. Invest time to review your actions, perhaps with your coach or advisor. Discover what worked best for you and any others you worked with or influenced during the achievement process.

That knowledge bodes well for the future. It'll save time, energy, and frustration as you set even bigger goals. You'll know you can do it, building more success using your previous success as the foundation.

Enjoying the payoff also sets an example of what can happen when you solidly stick to an objective, pouring yourself wholeheartedly into its accomplishment. Even if they don't quite understand everything you're doing, people are likely to respect you for your determination. Couple this with flexibility and insight in changing your attitude and actions in order to reach your goal, and you can't lose.

Consistent development of those leadership skills will benefit you as you move forward, challenging yourself to climb the next mountain. You'll attract others who like you and what you've become along the way. Your credibility will serve you and others well as you teach them through example—how to earn rewards and enjoy them, while always being on the grow!

7

New and Improved?

Somehow the advertising industry has determined that those two words must go together. The premise is that the only way to improve is to create something new. But is that always true? No, you don't need to reinvent something to make an improvement. That goes for your success at getting yes as well.

If all we did was throw everything away and start over every time we wanted something better, we'd all be at the beginning for much of our lives. (It wouldn't be very exciting being back in kindergarten, now would it?) While some things need to be totally redone in order to achieve a desired result, many of life's endeavors need only one or two minor adjustments to reach fruition. We don't have to reinvent the wheel.

When you're on a trip and encounter a detour, what do you do? Most people simply follow the new signs. An inconvenience for sure, but at least they know they'll get to where they want to go. Unfortunately, when people think they're going to fail after getting a no, many go all the way back home, instead of looking at it simply as a detour, only to quit. They give up on their relationship or quest, rather than forgiving or pressing on.

If you were going to meet with a new friend or prospect for the first time somewhere you've never been before, what would you do if you got lost? Go all the way back to the office and start the trip over? Probably not. You'd give him or her a call and ask for directions from wherever you were, or check your GPS (Global Positioning System), so you could get back on track and arrive at your destination. You may be a bit late, but you focused on your goal and achieved your objective. It was simple, but not in your original plan.

When expanding a manufacturing facility, is the original building torn down? Probably not. The improvement is often an addition to the current structure, enhancing its flexibility, capacity, and usefulness.

Challenges and noes always occur when you're in motion, heading for a destination. The road to success has bumps and unexpected encounters, and there's no exit to easy street. Detours and modifications may be necessary. Maybe one of your earlier approaches was faulty or you realized that what originally seemed like the hard way actually turned out to be the better way.

For example, it usually takes less time to get somewhere using the freeway, even though the mileage may be more than taking back roads. Adjustments could also be required as your needs and desires expand—possibly because of a life-changing epiphany.

Many people have a tendency to start from scratch every time they get a no. This lengthens or, at worst, stops the process of achievement, preventing them from gaining or sustaining momentum. Until they eliminate that habit, they're always going to hold their dream as a vague wish. This is sad, for yes is often just around the corner. Perhaps all that's needed is a little more patience and persistence, or the fine-tuning of a relationship or two.

Be Open to Suggestions and Assistance—*Use the Power of Synergistic Teamwork*

Having an open mind to incremental improvement is an attitudinal habit of those who get yeses. Just because you come up with an idea is no guarantee it'll work exactly, or even remotely, the way you think it will. However, giving it your all, and being humble in letting others who are in the know suggest improvements, can ultimately lead to more yeses.

My goal in writing this book was to share how to get yeses in a manner that would benefit most people. However, even though I gave it everything I had, no matter how focused I was or how sincere my intentions were, I may have missed an idea or presented something in a way that wasn't as understandable as it could have been. So I called on capable assistance—several pairs of eyes looking it over, brainstorming with me to make adjustments and fine tune. In working with others, I could thereby create considerably better results, a far superior product, than if I had just operated independently.

Ask successful authors and they'll tell you they couldn't have done what was required without the assistance of editors and proofreaders. The synergistic power of a team provides a multiplicative effect—much more powerful than each individual's contribution added up. The whole is greater than the sum of its parts! When a suggestion for improvement is made, a third and even better idea often emerges. While this obviously requires more work up-front, the results are always worth the effort.

Continue this synergistic process, consistently learning new things relative to your task. Incorporate refinements into your knowledge and attitude/skill set and get the mentoring you may need. You'll then be better able to help or serve others, while having a better sense in knowing when it's time to deliver the "goods," making it a priority, and doing it! Otherwise you put yourself through the perils of procrastination in a never-win situation, running the danger of not finishing the project nor achieving your objective. All who would have benefited are left in the dark. Who wants to live with that on their conscience? Not me! It's a chilling, complacency-shaking, wake-up call. This perspective has helped me press on when I didn't feel like writing yet another book, and it can spur you on too!

Few Things Are Final!

Once you commit to delivering your I'll-do-whatever-is-required effort, you may still feel frustrated. Not to worry. It's even okay to *feel* like quitting because the character you've developed by growing through no won't let you! You are now in gear, focusing on bringing your efforts to the world and meeting your objective.

> *"When an archer misses the mark, he turns and looks for the fault within himself. Failure to hit the bull's-eye is never the fault of the target. To improve your aim—improve yourself."*
>
> —GILBERT ARLAND

In this mode, you get other thoughts about improving what you thought was perfect—going for being better than your best—be it a book, presentation, product, report, service, or something else. I can't tell you how many times I've had thoughts regarding what I could have added to some of my previous books. I can't tell you the number of times a manuscript has been rewritten and re-edited. Yes, I've even felt like quitting.

When no happens, relax. Let it be. You're growing, and that's what matters. As in my case, it could lead to a whole new offering—just like the one you're now reading. Who knows? Rest assured, time and persistence toward getting yes will take you where you're supposed to go.

"Any supervisor worth his salt would rather deal with people who attempt too much than with those who try too little."

—LEE IACOCOA

8

Good Enough Is
Seldom Enough

any times when we're frustrated about an obstacle blocking our way to yes and we don't quite know how to handle it, someone will say, "Don't let it get the best of you." Unfortunately, upon hearing that, many people use it as an excuse to quit and walk away—retreating from the challenge rather than facing it.

Take a different approach with yourself and others. Whenever you engage in a new task, meet with a new situation, or simply do what you normally do every day, let the hurdles get the *better* of you. Do more. Plow through them. Blast through the obstacles as quickly as you can. Apply yourself fully.

What if it doesn't work out as you anticipated? Or you don't achieve the degree of success you aimed for? Did you honestly give it 100 percent? Was there something more you could have done with the level of awareness you had at the time? Congratulations! You've earned hindsight for the next time around. This can make a world of difference in your future outcomes.

Many people avoid the risk of having others point out their weaknesses. They sidestep the growth they would experience by failing to go at it again. They simply go about their lives in a typical status-quo, ho-hum pace. Many do just enough to get by, not making any waves. Their goal is to blend in rather than stand out, and they sure succeed at that. Observe their slouched postures, life's-a-drag walking styles, and unhappy resigned-to-carrying-burdens faces! Living an ordinary, not-going-for-it life filled with routine blandness and a lack of stimulating goals cannot be very exciting. These sad folks can easily be identified by their low energy, lackluster appearances. Have you ever known anyone like this?

This really isn't living. Wouldn't you agree? Becoming known for nothing unique or outstanding, vital, or significant by living an always-play-it-safe life is definitely not where it's at. If that's someone's desire, there's nothing wrong with that; they can go on doing what they're doing as long as it's providing them with the results they're after. However, they definitely lose the right to complain about the way things are. They may as well give up questioning the future as it is already set for them—more of the same or often worse. Unfortunately, they're foregoing the opportunities they have to shine and make a positive contribution, which could brighten others' lives as well as their own. Is that important to you? Hope so. It sure is to me.

What's the *BEST* that Could Happen?

One of my more popular programs is based on the power of setting goals. While this isn't the time to go through that, ask yourself, "What type of a goal would someone set who wants to just get by?"

I've asked that question many times and the response has often been something like, "I just want to make it to payday."

Those of you familiar with goal setting know that sometimes you just miss hitting a goal. But what would happen if you just missed a payday? Are you prepared for such a potentiality or would it be a small disaster? So what happens when you *make* a payday? Is it enough of a building block for the financial future you want? Or is it just keeping you stuck?

Goal setting asks you to stretch beyond what you've already accomplished, while giving renewed hope. Sure, it's disappointing if you don't achieve one, but resetting goals until you get them is always refreshing.

Until you accomplish them, ask yourself, "What mistakes did I make?" "What changes can I implement to help me get a yes?" "What compromises do I need to make?" This helps you regroup, refine your approach, and reset the goal. You're in the game. It all happens in the right time, even if it doesn't feel that way when you're going through it. Still skeptical?

Suppose you don't believe in setting goals. Or if asked, you say, "I just want to make it to payday." That's your goal. Okay. Now, suppose the ideas I've just shared work, and you barely missed your goal. Now what?

Suppose you make it to payday once again. What happens now? You've reached your goal. So what? Other than, hopefully, paying your bills, how is it helping you move forward? With a bottom-line goal of maintenance or survival, there's nothing to get excited about in achieving it, is there? This is a major reason for job dissatisfaction.

Think about it. It's one of the main reasons people work at maybe a number of jobs for decades, retire, if they can afford to, then spend the rest of their lives wondering, "Is this all there is?" They're not in the habit of setting new goals and working them through to completion. They give up at the first no. So what do they do? They might go out and get a second job! Now their time is totally gone, taken by two jobs they often begrudgingly work. But it's not because they don't have the brains or brawn to create the better life they really want either! What's wrong with this picture?

Imagine going through life hitting every single goal you ever set. But because of the lackluster nature of your goals, you aimed so low that you never really felt good about what you accomplished. Granted, they were achieved, but you always seemed to stay on neutral ground—neither here nor there. So what have you become?

I often refer to this situation as "settling in to settling for." Instead of working toward and creating the life they honestly desire, some people simply accept what happens as if it's a part of some master plan they have no control over. If you get, you get; if you don't, you don't. No point in getting riled up about it; that's just the way it is. Their friends, all in the same boat with the same attitude, nod their heads in agreement: "So, so" (Same old, same old) they mumble in unison, in their all-too-familiar monotone way.

But now let's assume you joined a different group. What if you woke up one day saying, "I've had enough. I'm fed up. I'm sick and tired of the status quo. Nothing's getting better. I'm ready to make a change"?

What's the worst that could happen? A no? Have *you* ever said no to anyone or anything else? Sure! Noes are part of life.

Dwelling on the potential of no stops people from advancing toward yes. They focus on the obstacle, no, instead of the objective, yes! It makes them think of how everyone will react if they don't achieve success. Once they discover most people don't care, it may be too late. It deludes them into thinking maybe they're better off just going along to get along, but the boredom of it all continues to plague them. The idea of having their tombstone read, "Here lie Mr. and Mrs. Mediocrity, they barely paid their bills," doesn't thrill them either.

Suppose we alter the question a little, changing *worst* to *best*, as in—"What's the *best* that could happen?" Imagine a situation or a yes you'd like to achieve. Focus on it until you visualize and believe it's happening. Ask yourself, "What's the best that could happen?" and wait for the answer. Is it an improved situation? Would that be worth going through the noes? You bet. I dare you to do it!

No Is Part and Parcel of the Process of Success

How do you feel? Are you getting stirred up? Are you beginning to think a little differently now? Instead of imagining everything that can go wrong—getting noes—you accept them as a natural part of the success process. You begin seeing the one thing that keeps you going—the possibilities for yes. You believe yes *is* possible, even in your darkest moments. This can work wonders on every aspect of your thinking and attitude— your whole way of thinking about yourself and others.

As you see a desired scenario as possible, as a yes, doesn't it make you feel more confident? You come alive with hope for the future and start smiling more. You realize there's a whole new range of potential yeses just waiting for you to find them. You claim the yeses as yours. You're feeling more confident already, aren't you? What kind of person do you see yourself becoming as you achieve more yeses? Do you find people attracted to you because of your fresh *new* outlook on things?

This pivotal change, this mind shift, as long as it's fed, supported, and sustained, always results in a multitude of positive results. People who can help you are now attracted to you rather than put off by your previous no attitude. Your relationships shine as you move forward. You let go of any cynicism, forgive yourself and others readily and graciously, realizing we're all in this together. You're also producing higher quality work in your family, community, and work. You feel stronger, finding yourself consistently going the extra mile, not worrying about the results. You know you'll persist until you get that yes. You've made it a habit. You realize your attitude toward everyone and everything is transforming your life, reigning supreme in achieving yes.

Did You Ever Get a Paycheck from a Poor Person?

One of the challenges of taking on a What's-the-BEST-thing-that-could-happen? attitude could be your pressuring yourself about what others might be thinking. Many times, the first concern is how those around you would react or respond. You might start hearing them say things that cause you to waiver. They might be insecure and not want you to move ahead of them. All it may be, though, is that they're simply afraid of no!

Remember, none of the people who try to hold you back or pull you down will be there to help you meet your obligations or accomplish your goals. While they may do everything they can to prevent you from going after your objective—laugh at you, reject you, and the like—rest assured none will volunteer to make the additional income you need if you choose to stay where you are. They may have adopted an I'd-just-like-to-make-it-to-payday attitude, creating an unnecessarily small and unexciting life. How sad.

> *"The man who wins may have been counted out several times, but he didn't hear the referee."*
>
> —H. E. JANSEN

Any success I've been blessed with has come from reaching out and learning from those who had already accomplished what I wanted to do—those who were in the position I aspired to. To become better at sales, I hung out with the best salesperson on staff and did what they did. When I wanted to get a promotion to management, I learned from those who were already there, going beyond the call of duty, proving I could handle the elevated role. On the writing front, since the majority of writers simply give up before they're ever published, I could have counted my blessings just to see my name in print. But when I became an entrepreneur and wanted my books to sell, I hung around bestselling authors and learned by their example.

I'm no whiz kid and no better than you are. I'm a pretty regular human being, with ups and downs just like everyone else. However, I habitually get back up, over and over again. It's a habit that's essential for anyone who's 100 percent flat out going for his or her objective. Nonetheless, at each of the previous steps of my chosen path, certain people wanted to "protect" me from myself and my aspirations. They wanted to shield me from being disappointed, as they might have been when they quit short of the mark. Basically, they wanted me not to go beyond them. To be honest, it wasn't all bad but it *could* have been, had I let them negatively influence me. They showed me how *not* to be and act! To be honest, the thought of backing off sometimes felt like a relief, but I could never bring myself to give up on my dream. How about you?

Not being a top salesperson initially meant no one would pressure me to "pull out the month" when things were down. By not being in management I could have blended in with the crowd and not have to take the blame for the department's overall lack of performance. The problem in both cases was that the lack of responsibility would have meant three things:

1. Never being on the edge of making a big win.
2. Never having productive discussions with anyone to work through the challenges.
3. Never having Cheshire-cat-like grins when, as a team, we finally hit the mark.

But I *really* wanted to be *the* top salesperson, and I knew the only way was to do whatever it took—to accept noes as part and parcel of the game. After all, no one was about to reward me with something I didn't earn. I wanted to lead a team of people toward great success. I wanted to be a champion. When I went out on my own as an author and speaker, I was committed to seeing my books reach the highest numbers of people so they could be helped by the lessons I've learned. I wanted to make a greater difference by sharing my hard knocks so they could be put to greater use by helping others along on their path.

Those were some of the possibilities I saw for the efforts I was making, instead of taking a backseat, looking out the window at someone else's success. I imagined what it would feel like to be a leader of a successful team and saw the gratifying results of putting others first. I realized that if I spent most of my time working hard to help others succeed, rather than worrying about where I stood among my peers, my success was virtually guaranteed.

"Do not wish to be anything but what you are, and endeavor to be that perfectly."

—St. Francis de Sales

9

So What's So Good About You?

Sometimes we let false modesty cloud our accomplishments. Not giving ourselves any credit for a job well done, or for taking a risk that benefited others, might cause us to be reluctant to tackle something like that again.

This would be quite unfortunate for ourselves and others. It may cause others in need of what we have to offer to unnecessarily look elsewhere, when we could have had a great solution to their situation or desire. Even if we've been in the game just long enough to make a home run, we need to let others know how we did it. If we don't speak up, how can what we've learned and done possibly help anyone else?

There's everything right with being good at something as long as we do the right thing. Contributing value through incremental accomplishment is not only a natural component of success, it's also essential for continued growth.

No one is self made. It's okay to acknowledge what you've achieved, as long as you humbly recognize those who have helped you along the way and share with others how you did it. How else could you go to the next level in whatever you're doing? How could you possibly maximize your potential and be better equipped to create a difference, if you don't share what you did with anyone else—consistently selling yourself and your accomplishments short? What if you do the same to others who are put in your midst, however briefly, to touch? It's essential to be humble, but underrating yourself doesn't serve anyone.

Can you imagine trying to put together a championship team when no one has more than an inkling that he or she has anything on the ball or worthy of notice? What if everyone has a losing mentality, where no one strives to give it their all? How do you determine who plays when no one thinks they're any good? It doesn't work. Translate this to winning yeses in life—they come only to those who earn them, by growing through the noes. Shirking responsibilities gets us nowhere. It's stretching and assuming responsibilities that'll take us to the next level. Saying yes to a brighter future always comes through no!

Each of us is unique and has a special combination of qualities and personal history that's absolutely our own. While some may be as good as or better than we are at various things, our heartfelt inclinations and desires are ours alone. We certainly have human nature woven into our makeup, giving us many similar threads. But to put ourselves down in any way by saying, "I'm only one person" (welcome to the club!) just creates an excuse—rather than an achievement-filled environment. This is only a disservice to both ourselves and others.

To acquire a reputation for being the best at something, take on challenging situations, like noes, full speed ahead. Demonstrate your mettle over and over again and make the champion within you known. Even when it seems like you can't handle one more no, blast through it—whatever it takes. It's okay to feel like quitting, but never okay to do. Noes build character, determining what you're made of. Show them!

No One Is Self-Made, *But It's Important to Be Recognized*

Many people shy away from recognition, often feeling reticent about accepting accolades. Somehow they feel they don't deserve it. But have you ever considered that by saying yes to the spotlight, where your triumphs are highlighted, you can help get others pumped up for moving on and making an even greater difference? Have you ever considered that choosing anonymity could actually hurt someone who sorely needs your example to follow and give them hope? Believe me, they're out there, and this is your chance to reach them. There's one thing better than living the dream and that's sharing it with others!

How about the individuals, families, programs, companies, or organizations that could be helped by your graciously accepting compliments and appreciation, while sharing what you've gone through to get where you are? Even though you didn't do it for the glory or recognition, and may have been surprised by it, kindly accept the smiles, admiration, and applause. Others benefited from your actions and it is their gift back to you. It brightens their spirits and gives them inspiration and pleasure in acknowledging you.

"The point is to develop the childlike desire for recognition and to guide the child."

—ALBERT EINSTEIN

After I speak in front of a large group, the host invariably presents me with a gift. They might give it to me after I finish talking, or they could choose not to give me anything at all. In most cases, they ask me to remain on stage for a formal presentation. After experiencing this over and over again, I thought it might be a good idea to welcome it as a multifaceted prize, more meaningful than initially meets the eye. It's gratifying all the way around—the bestowing, receiving, and observing. Since it uplifts everyone there and beyond through the ripple effect we all have, we want our influence to be a good one! An individual shining in the light of contribution has undoubtedly teamed up with others to get it done.

It's what you do to exert positive change that earns the really important prize. So how about striving for it every time you go out to accomplish something? How about consistently working as if you're going for the top award? How about pulling out all stops, considering the example you'll be to others, fully recognizing the coach or mentor who helped you get there? Remember, you get nothing unless you perform all the things that make you deserving of the reward, and you don't get there by yourself—no one does. True enough, some accomplishments appear to be solitary endeavors. Upon closer examination, however, certain behind-the-scenes people and elements had to come together. No one is self-made! It may sound good, but don't ever be fooled by it.

Risk No and Failure—*It's the Only Way to Yes and Success!*

What fun is there in stagnation? If you question that, take a look at the stuck souls around you. Are they having any fun? I don't think so.

Are you serious about becoming the person you were meant to be, striving for the life you want to live? Constantly do what moves you in the direction of your objective—the tasks and situations, like the potential for no, that cause you to stretch and grow. Since success won't just fall into your lap, earn and pave your way to the front of the line. Boldly step out and take on responsibilities that go beyond the call of duty. Create new forward-moving habits, demonstrating what you can really do, while setting a shining example for others.

Most of the world is simply too busy to keep track of you and what you're good at. If you've been keeping your strengths a secret, it's not likely you'll have as many opportunities to show what you can do. Roll up your sleeves and help others. Make yourself a more reliable asset. Watch your popularity rise as you rigorously take an interest in others and serve them, and watch your income likely rise as well. Jump into the game and give it all you've got—*over and over again.* That's how winners get good at what they do.

There's another key component to growing and developing. It's called taking risks. Start a new initiative and take action, in spite of any fears you may have. Know, going in, that there's the possibility that what you're about to attempt may not work out as desired. You could "fail"—you could get a no!

But, that's okay. Unless you take action where you risk failure and no, there's no possible way for you to ever achieve more than average results. It's as simple as that. Go out there and expose yourself to the possibility of no and failure, and you'll open yourself up to the possibility for yes and success. That's just how it works in the world of achievers. You can't have one without the possibility of the other. We've all got to deal with it, even the most emulated go-getters on earth. Especially them! They're not on top by accident.

While you're risking the possibility of no, dismiss any idea of doing it haphazardly. Do it thoughtfully. Jump in the game as quickly as you can. Dwelling on the preparation phase plummets you into the ditch of grey everydayness, where wishes never turn into objectives or reality. Go with what you have. There's no time to waste. Every second counts!

Yes, preparation helps you reduce the chance of failure and no, but doesn't eliminate it. We're all in the same boat on this one. It's just part of the game. If you do everything within your power to make something work, asking for assistance when needed, and still get a no, it's only a temporary setback. Reflect briefly on what you did and make appropriate changes.

As ironic as it may sound, the opportunity to fine-tune is a major benefit of failing or being told no. Choose to become better rather than bitter; it makes you stronger. Shorten your learning curve by taking full advantage of the lessons no teaches. The key is to continue learning from no, starting again where you left off. Then go for it, always ready to succeed in the next round, until you ring the bell of victory.

One of the main distinctions between those who have enjoyed massive success and those who haven't, are the number of times they've heard no and failed. They're constantly tweaking themselves and their approach, while continuing to expose themselves to the possibility of even more noes or failings. Always look at them as the way to yes and succeeding! You can't grow unless you're out there with the winners getting noes, failing your way to success.

"Faith is the daring of the soul to go farther than it can see."

—AUTHOR UNKNOWN

10

Understand, *"They"* Probably Aren't Thinking About You!

Remember those wonderful teen years? Anytime you wanted to do something you were certain your parents would forbid, you called on your buddies. You know who I mean. You called them by various names: they, everyone else, no one," and the like. As adults, these all meld into one— The Committee of They—often unconsciously holding court on how you form your decisions.

What would *they* do? How would *they* feel? What would *they* say? What would *they* think? Sound familiar? Some people spend so much time justifying their decisions, actions, and results based on *they* that these folks rarely accomplish much of anything significant. And yet, all the law enforcement entities in the world can't even identify who *they* are.

How many people have let *they* rule their lives, forcing themselves to make ill-informed, failure generating, poor decisions? When someone comes up with a plan or an opportunity to make life better, why does what *they* think, feel, say, or do often enter and cloud the picture? Most people are more concerned about what the mysterious *they* characters think than what they themselves personally think! It's a sad situation often leading to the consequences of countless missed opportunities for improving life—causing closed mindedness, risk aversion, or complete risk refusal.

The reality is, *they* are generally too busy with their own concerns to care about what we do or don't do. As shocking, disconcerting, or disappointing as this may sound, it's freeing when you really stop to think about it. Why are we so concerned about what other people think when most of them aren't on the path we chosen? Frankly, *they* really don't care, one way or the other, what you're up to. *They* are all caught up in their own stuff. Ironically, *they* are worrying about what the world is thinking about *them*. *They* are self-absorbed, with no room in their lives to really pay any attention to how *you* dress, what *you* think, or if *you* have any plans to better your life in any way.

> *"The people who get in on this world are those who get up and look for circumstances they want, and if they can't find them, make them."*
>
> —GEORGE BERNARD SHAW

Sorry to disappoint you, but the people you think are thinking about you probably aren't! Since we are all responsible for our own lives, chances are really good no one else is paying our bills. This leaves us free to make the decisions we need to create the life we want!

Right Is Right—*Even Without a Witness*

Unfortunately, many people today are more concerned about protecting themselves from risk or no than in improving their lives. They don't want to rock the boat for fear of disapproval or dismissal. Instead of working toward making things better or doing a better job, many are simply doing what limits their exposure to potential criticism, doing only what they absolutely have to do to get by. This results in not meeting quality standards and an increase in job dissatisfaction. Surveys show that most people aren't happy with their job or some aspect of their employment situation.

Imagine how sad it must be if our biggest reason for not giving it a 100 percent is to avoid the jealousy or resentment of others. Then, when a company decides enough is enough and trims the fat, those who were leaning on the system are amazed when they're let go, demanding, "Why me?" as if they had nothing to do with it.

What if you worked as though you owned the place? Would you be the first one out the door when everyone else goes home, or would you stay behind to make sure everything was done? Do you spend time wondering how you can get a raise without any extra effort, or are you putting in extra effort without even a thought of getting paid? Do you dread Monday and wish for the weekend, or are you disappointed at how soon Friday shows up?

Suppose you acted as if you *did* own the place. You showed up early to get yourself ready for the day's work, and began your day focused. You kept on-task rather than looking at the clock, out the window, or sneaking in personal calls, Internet visits, or emails. You conducted yourself as if the entire company depended on you so payroll could be met and a profit made. What do you suppose could happen?

Even if no one ever realized what you were doing, you'd still be rewarded. Did you ever notice that when you're totally committed, sold-out to something, time is no longer an issue? When you focus everything on doing your job as well as you can, the days just fly by. You find yourself wanting to spend more time at work so you can accomplish even more. You aren't concerned about your time off or a vacation because you don't need to vacate something you enjoy. You're excited to be making things happen—it's your joy.

But it's highly unlikely your efforts would go unnoticed; others in power will probably see what you're doing. When tough decisions have to be made, you're more likely to be favored. Perhaps you'll get a raise or a promotion. Or, when things need to be cut back, you'll survive it. Why? Because in many companies today, doing a job better on self-initiative alone is becoming rare.

All that aside, giving it your maximum effort is a great habit. Whether you get to stay at a job you enjoy, pursue another opportunity, or retire, when you give something your all it's easy to focus on the future rather than trying to protect yourself from the past. Once something becomes a habit, whether it's an attitude or action, you do it automatically.

If you can give it a 100 percent while no one is watching, you'll have no problem making the right decision when someone *is*. You'll evaluate from a position of "What's the right thing to do?" rather than "What will others think?"

Credibility and Responsibility

Credibility is critical to success. Whether you're in sales, working toward a promotion, or running your own business, it's what people *don't* have to think about that can make all the difference. When others are considering you, especially for something important, whether it's a partnership or a promotion, their first thoughts about you will heavily influence the outcome.

Let's say your intention is to leave your job and go into business for yourself. In seeking clients, customers, patients, or people to team up with, wouldn't it be easier if you had credibility rather than spending the majority of your time trying to convince them to listen to what you have to say?

Is your reputation that of someone who's always giving everything your all, *never* leaving anyone holding the bag? Do you *always* take full responsibility, and beyond, for all your actions? If you're known for these attributes, you're building credibility.

Credibility is powerful when you don't have to explain it, when there's no pretense, just facts and solidity. When people know you are all you say you are and sense your integrity, your focus is simple. Explain the benefits of what you have to offer, honestly and thoroughly dealing with any objections they may have, and let people decide if it fits them—whether it's yes, no, or maybe. Without credibility, you have to defend why people should even consider listening to you let alone evaluate your offer.

This doesn't mean you have to already be highly experienced or tremendously successful with what you're presenting. You may just be at the onset of what you're doing, and have little experience. That's okay. Go with what you've got. You may have to defer to someone else's credibility on that score. That's okay too. But always be rock solid dependable and sincerely care about others, or you'll lose. You can fool people for a while but you'll get found out sooner or later. So go in clean from the beginning.

Most business activities, whether sales, consideration for advancement, expansion, or something else, are based on relationships. For example, even when a superior doesn't really know you all that well, they base their decision on what they *don't* have to consider—the likelihood of you not being able to handle the job. They already know you put a 100 percent into everything you do. They can count on you doing what's best for them and the company. If you make an error, you learn from it, make it right, and keep going.

If you're looking to develop a business relationship, your firm commitment will show through in your presentation. Your integrity and confidence will shine. Sureness rather than doubt will be obvious. People will sense your sincerity, your genuineness.

If you've already demonstrated your commitment in the past in doing whatever it takes to make something a success, it becomes easier for others to say yes to you. The offer would stand on its own merits, rather than be tangled up with whether or not you would be someone they want to purchase from or be associated with.

Simple Helps Success Along

By now you realize I don't offer much in the way of complicated solutions. Making something tough to understand only makes it easier for others to say no and give up. My take is to do what's simple, and you're more likely to get a yes. But don't be fooled. Simple doesn't necessarily mean easy.

The simplest reason for giving a 100 percent effort is because it's the right thing to do. Spend your life doing the right thing and you won't have the regret of ill-intention, which only causes remorse and failure. Your stress level will be low, too, and you'll never have to remember how you acted or what you said, because it was based on the truth. Any mistakes you might make would be unintentional. If you find out later your understanding or action was wrong, you apologize and make restitution. In the final analysis, you do the right thing even if it costs you. It'll pay off in the long run.

Simple solutions help you get yeses and keep you on the path of the life you want to live. Your goals are easier to set when they're not bogged down by the complications of how to achieve them. They won't be laden with excuses as to why you can't either. Clarity is dominant, and challenges are worked through without creating unnecessary hurdles.

Going for simple solutions eliminates the tired explanations needed when things don't go well, increasing your chances for yes. You'll never have to avoid answering a question by saying "It's too complicated to explain," only to be told no.

> *"Genius is the ability to reduce the complicated to the simple."*
>
> —C. W. CERNAN

> *"Restlessness is discontent—and discontent is the first necessity of progress. Show me a thoroughly satisfied man, and I will show you a failure."*
>
> —Thomas Edison

11

Committed to Getting Yes but Conditioned to Accepting No

We all want more success. You probably bought this book hoping to find a path that would lead you to more yeses, and the success you've always dreamed of. While the results you produce from reading it remain to be seen, you may already be better off than you think.

When does success actually occur? If you're aiming to be slim and trim, are you a success only after the last ounce is shed? If you want to quit smoking, are you a success when you no longer crave a cigarette? The answer to these questions is a resounding "No!"

Is Success the End Point—*or Something Else?*

Success is typically considered to have been accomplished only upon the completion of a task. That's what's most obvious and generally recognized and remembered. But is that *really* what success is all about? The end point? No! Real success is different. Understanding that may be exactly what you need to keep going when things get tough. Knowing when you first start becoming more successful helps you maintain the right mental attitude. It helps you persist in spite of what's happening at any given moment. "But when does that occur?" you ask.

Success is really a *process* that begins the instant you commit and take appropriate action—rather than just at the moment of accomplishment, as wonderful as that is. The instant you firmly decide to accomplish something and begin taking action in that direction, you're in the process of being more successful. Not being clear on this one concept keeps many from even making the effort to better themselves. They look at the big chunk of cheese rather than the small bites it takes to eat it!

Look at it from a different angle. Suppose you believe I'm wrong and think you need to accomplish what you set out to do in order to be a success. How would you react to the following scenario?

Let's say you set the goal of becoming a millionaire, for all the right reasons. You vow to do whatever it takes to realize it. You take action and your projected date for its accomplishment arrives. You call your financial consultant to see if you've made it yet. He tallies the results and says, "Oh, my gosh, you're not there yet—you only have $999,999.99!" Yes, *mathematically*, you've failed. That's an irrefutable fact. The goal was numerical and you thought it had to be accomplished before you could consider yourself a success. But, if you believed this, then every missed goal, no matter how close you get, makes you a failure. This is dangerous thinking and keeps many from striving to reach their true potential.

To fall one cent short is a numerical failure for sure. An extreme example, yes, but it makes the point that the journey is the success. Success begins when you say yes to yourself, commit to the task, and take action. If you haven't yet reached your goal, reset the target date as many times as needed and keep going. That's not only okay, but a normal part of the process of getting yes! You're becoming more successful *in the process*. You're growing. Your success in life is not just results based, even though society may look at it that way. Success is commitment and action based—you're developing as a person and achieving goals incrementally. The real benefit of setting and achieving goals is what they cause you to become in the process. This journey itself is the success!

Regardless of the goals you're setting and how far you're along in achieving them, what matters most is that you care about others, and are helping them grow and have a better life. Every contribution characterizes who you are and what you stand for. It could be that you're a greeter somewhere and give everyone who comes in the door a big grin! Or maybe you have something to offer people that can make a long-lasting positive impact on their lives, regardless of how many people say no in between the yeses.

Nothing Makes No Feel Good—*But It Has a Benefit!*

Nothing I can write, say, or do will ever make no feel good to you. I still don't like it when it happens to me. Who does? Nevertheless, rejection always has its benefits. As long as we keep plugging away with focus, it leads to a new direction. It's the attitude of a person on track to get a yes. So how do I deal with the queasy feeling I get when a no creeps into my plans? I simply allow a few seconds for the natural feeling of disappointment to come and then dissipate. I don't dwell on it or let it hold me back. I move on. Be more determined and pick up the pace.

> *"Never let a setback become a holdback."*
> —THE PUBLISHER

Hark back to something you've already accomplished that's significant to you. Think back to the time when you decided to go for it. Was there any time during the goal-achieving process that you calculated just how many noes you anticipated you'd hear before you got the yeses that lead to success? You had a firm grip on what you were looking to do and focused on getting yes. Maybe you thought about the benefits of growing and becoming more than you were. Think about how much your attitude has improved as well as your ability to meet and deal with situations. Think about how you're growing in taking risks and creating new relationships, and how you've developed as a person. All priceless gains, all priceless yeses.

As long as you continue to hold your objective as bigger in your mind than the obstacles you meet along the way, you'll keep going. If you focus on the noes, they'll take on more importance in your mind and, eventually, block the sight of yes and your destination. You get what you focus on; pure and simple.

If you feel a bit hurt or let down by a no or disappointed by a failing, it's just part of being in the human race and it's okay. Allow a little time to process those feelings, but only grant yourself a brief break in the action—take a few minutes, an hour, or even a day, depending on the situation. Have you ever been to a party that lasted forever? Well, pity parties shouldn't either. Place a time limit on yourself. Don't dwell on it. Get back up, dust yourself off, and get back in the race. Have the attitude that says, "I'm up or I'm getting up!" Winners keep moving. They're committed to getting yes.

The Powerful Question of a Three-Year-Old

Parents, remember saying these things? "Come over here," you demand. The response, "Why?" "Because I said so," you continue. And on it goes. "Why?" is such a powerful question. It's also timeless. Start asking "why?" like you did of your Mom and Dad when you were only three. But now ask it of yourself.

"Why?" gives you energy. When you know why you are working toward something, it's easier to stay committed when the going gets tough. When you have a reason for doing something, the work never seems as hard as it otherwise might. No just doesn't matter anymore—you know you'll get through it all and win those yeses—as long as you don't quit.

Look at people who are happy at their work and always seem to have the right attitude. They smile, wink, whistle, or sing, no matter what challenge they're facing, knowing, as Abe Lincoln said, "This, too, shall pass." If you were to speak to them, you'll likely find that they have a good reason, a why, for doing what they're doing. They see themselves as getting somewhere or attaining something. They do their best to make a difference. They know they'll be more productive by maintaining a great attitude. It's essential for a happy life. If you find yourself slipping into a negative state, switch gears by looking for the good.

While people often work the same number of hours for the same income, what each accomplishes can be entirely different. One can be providing more options for their family, while the other might be working more with no end in sight, finding it a drag. Why has the power to give you an inspired purpose.

Imagine someone who says he's been looking to make a positive change in his life, yet tells you he's too busy when the opportunity comes along. The truth is anyone who's doing anything to speak of is busy. To help them get beyond that, they simply need a strong enough why. As the old saying goes, "If you want something done, ask a busy person." Ask someone with a big enough why and they'll say yes!

"Let him who would move the world first move himself."
—SOCRATES

The next time you're deciding whether or not to take on a certain task, ask yourself "Why?" Why would you want to do it? What's your reason? Come up with a positive why for yourself, get started, and you'll find the task goes more quickly and doesn't seem as difficult. Your attitude will be contagious and attract others to you. Shift your attitude and home in on whatever target is beckoning your attention.

"The competitor to be feared is the one who never bothers about you at all, but goes on making his own business better all the time."

—HENRY FORD

12

Competitive Participation Creates Ongoing Acceleration

Competition can occur on two levels—conscious and unconscious. Conscious competition is easier to identify and work with; people can tell you about it. They could be in the same line of work trying to land the same clients and customers. They could be bidders on the property you'd like to own. Simply asking someone who they think their competition is easily identifies this type.

Unconscious competition is created by conditioning. You're competing against what people have become used to in their everyday lives. You have to work against these unidentified competitors; sometimes never knowing who or what they are.

In the insurance industry, for example, when someone wants a quote for a policy, it may take more than an instant to get an answer—sometimes days. While the agent may be working to make certain the right information and price is delivered, unconscious competition may be causing the prospect to look elsewhere.

Why would somebody who may rarely need new insurance react that way? Is it impatience, anxiety—the desire to have information now? Could be. What conditions cause people to be dissatisfied with the time it takes to get answers? Could being able to go on the Internet and, in a matter of seconds, receive mortgage quotes from several lenders, or apply for and be approved for a credit card in less than five minutes? So why can't the insurance industry provide instant answers?

The reality of insurance is that many factors go into certain policies, increasing the length of time needed for providing accurate numbers. We may be fully aware that instantaneous or relatively quick acquisition of our desired results is not reasonable to anticipate. This may be a fact of whatever industry or organization we're in. But, regardless, unconscious competition can cause us to move irrationally toward another company, situation, or opportunity when we're not getting what we want as soon as we want. Some people have a habit of running away from their objective acquisition process as soon as expectations aren't met; doing it over and over again. It's like being on a treadmill, running nowhere except to frustration and complaint land, where most people live.

Be *Really* in the Game!

Many people shun competition because with it comes the possibility of no and failing. In business, someone has to get the account; in school, one is chosen valedictorian; in the movies there can only be one best picture of the year; in sports, there's only one championship winning team in each genre.

But, considering the odds, one thing's for certain: *Playing the game* is the only way to even have a chance for yes! If you sit out at every opportunity, technically, you can't get a no and lose. But in reality, you do lose, as you have nothing to win. So where does that leave you? Is that where you want to be? No, of course not! You must prepare for yes. You must study to excel. If you're not willing to risk the potential for no and follow through with guts and gumption, you have no chance at coming out on top or getting a yes. You never even entered the game. You're still sitting on the sidelines, never mind being suited up.

However, the real key to playing the game is to humbly learn, being totally teachable, as you institute the required changes for lasting success. Participate as a passionate player, rising to the next challenge. Always learn something new to make yourself better, while teaching others to do the same in preparing for the next opportunity "on the field." Winners breed winners. Even when you come out on top, constant improvement is necessary to continue at that level. You can count on the existing competition to improve, or new competition to enter the scene, no matter what you do or don't do. Stay on the cutting edge, constantly striving to make your mark.

It's extremely rare that an attempt, invention, or new concept is ready for victory the first time out. It's usually a process combining time and experience—coupled with noes, flexibility, and action—while making improvements.

> *"He can who thinks he can, and he can't who thinks he can't. This is an inexorable indisputable law."*
> —ORISON SWETT MARDEN

When I'm working with a sales training client, I encourage them to spend as little of their time and money as possible on the actual closing of deals. While focusing on the closing many neglect the process and the groundwork to get there. Sure it can be fun just envisioning the prize and staying in the dream zone; it's safe and secure. You can't get pounced by the competition by staying in the audience, passively watching the performance. Unless you are an extra on a movie set, though, you don't get paid to be in the audience! Closing deals, getting yeses, happens only when the right relationships are made and the groundwork laid. Spending too much time imagining the results without putting what we're learning into action tends to produce little reward, and a lot of noes!

When you watch athletes, what usually happens at the end of a great event? The top competitors typically shake hands or give each other some other form of acknowledgment. They understand their opponent may have done their best, but on this particular day it wasn't quite enough. Did you ever seek out someone who did better than you just to congratulate them? Why not? Let go of any ego and do it—congratulate, then emulate! In baseball, when hitters get together, even when they play for different teams, they talk about hitting. They all share what works for them, and how they go about preparing for a particular pitcher.

Suppose you sat with your biggest competitor and compared notes. What might you learn? You may find that you're on the right track and they beat you only in cases where they lowered their price to a point where little profit was made. You might discover they spend a great deal of time learning as much about your products as they do about their own. If such an idea would be ethical, you could even explore the possibility of someday merging and working together. But, rest assured, as long as you were both honorable, neither of you would come out of the meeting worse off than before you went in. Instead, you'd have a whole new outlook on your competition, even looking forward to your next encounter as friendly contenders. There's room for everybody.

Competitive Participation Creates *Ongoing Acceleration*

Anyone who has ever participated in an event with at least one other participant has competed. If you ask most of them what it was like, they would tell you it made them better. The experience opened their minds to quick and creative thinking and, for those who rose to excellence, superlative performance.

When you strategically plan for a game, a sales presentation, or even something personal, you take into account what you know and formulate a plan of action. For some, working on that plan reveals possible pitfalls, often leaving them stuck at that stage. Rather than beefing up their stick-with-it stamina and applying more energy, they quit when a potential obstacle, or no, looms. They ignore the golden chance to ask for guidance, while persisting until they figure out how to best handle it. They're the first to make excuses, whining and complaining about their objective as being impossible to accomplish. They talk to others who failed at it, too, commiserating, drowning their sorrows. What they don't realize is that anything we set out to accomplish, if we haven't done it before, typically looks challenging. Why? We haven't done it before! We're simply not experienced at doing it!

So, keep your original goal solidly in mind—as you're developing a plan of action. For best results, do it in concert with someone who knows more about it than you. Immerse yourself in the process. Be flexible so you can end up with an improved way of achieving it. Regularly supercharge yourself by focusing on your objective and it'll help you maintain momentum.

Yes! Competitive participation creates ongoing acceleration. When you're in motion, when you're in friendly competition, your mind sharpens and works at an increased pace. This enables you to see and take advantage of opportunities to move forward, and tune into possibilities faster than when you're just in the planning mode, sitting still. When you are thoroughly engaged in the activity, you become more confident in the trial-and-error tweaking process. Use momentum to propel you, while fine-tuning your actions as needed. If you prove to yourself you are using the wrong tact, regroup and keep moving.

"Failures are divided into two classes—those who thought and never did, and those who did and never thought."
—JOHN CHARLES SALAK

Even when you've made a mistake, your activity level helps you more quickly assess the situation, remedy it, or adjust and move on. This type of get-over-it-and-get-on-with-it thinking can only occur when you're active in body, mind, and spirit. You can't plan around it or take it into account as long as you're still in the preparation stage. You can only modify on the fly! Nothing can be guided until it's in motion. Let go of waiting for things to be perfect. View it as perfect right now, including what may seem like imperfection. What's perfect for one person may not be for another. Business and life are full of imperfections and change. It's a fact of life, whether we like it or not; we just need to accept it and keep moving.

People often lock into the planning or preparation stage, trying to take every possibility into account. But too much can happen for that to work. Put your plan into action, rethinking it along the way.

If you don't participate, if you don't compete, how can you expect to win? Truly winning is about friendly competition and ongoing participation. It's about getting in there, getting dirt on your hands, and passionately playing the game. Winning and losing can occur only for players. Everyone else is just taking up space. Life is not a spectator sport. You've got to make it happen. Remember, competitive participation creates ongoing acceleration.

"If you want to be enthusiastic, act enthusiastic. Inner enthusiasm follows."

—WILLIAM ELLIS

13

Enthusiasm Is Essential and Contagious

Shortly before *Reject Me—I Love It!* was published, I was in dire straits. I had been working on the book straight for nearly six months; income from my consulting work had virtually disappeared; and there appeared to be no end in sight. I dwelled on my financial stress rather than staying in my creative zone and finishing the book. This, of course, delayed any chance of income from its sales or speaking engagements. It felt like I had been given a big thud on the chest—as if I had been told a big fat no!

I spent a lot of time locked in my office, with thoughts of how bad things were. It was tough being a husband and father believing I had no answers. The more I consternated about it, wallowing in the mud of self-pity, the less I was able to focus on getting the book done. My eyes were solely looking on myself and my situation. My losing attitude caused a downward mental spiral, making matters appear worse. More and more negative thoughts piling up on one another made things look even bleaker. The mountain of obstacles in my mind was blocking my view of the objective. I was in danger of losing the dream. A vicious cycle was beginning to ensue.

Even though I had taught my children the importance of having dreams and goals, I was thinking about the pitfalls rather than the possibilities. I was a poor example for the kids. I was too busy being caught up in a web of tangled misconceptions, focused on just getting by, merely surviving, getting through the day, the week. Then my son strode confidently into the office.

"Dad," he said, grinning broadly, "I want to play baseball for Florida State University." Even though he was only eleven at the time, his clarity was amazing. It jolted me out of the doldrums. There was no way I was going to steal his dream. I had to get out of my funk. I smiled right back and told him that if I had to sell books door to door, I would finish this one and get him to the school of his choice. Big mistake!

He instantly ran upstairs to tell his five-year-old sister he was going to Florida. To a five year old, there's only one thing in Florida—Disney World. My daughter got upset. She ran to her mother, crying, "How come Daddy's taking Johnny to Disney World? I want to go too. Why can't I go?" And on it went.

My wife was a little taken aback. So she did what parents typically do in that situation. She sent our daughter marching right to my office to ask me herself.

By the time Katie came to me, feeling I was really in a pickle now, I was ready to pack it in and go back to looking for a job. But when she came bursting through the door, all smiles, so excited, breathlessly asking, "Daddy, are you taking us to Disney World?" I told her, if that was her dream then it was my job to make it come true. Bigger mistake.

She couldn't get up the stairs any faster than if she had flown. Right to her mother she went, telling her we were all going to Disney because Daddy said so.

My wife knew everything that was going on. She couldn't possibly see how we could ever get to Disney with the situation as it was. Yet, she knew I would never lie to the kids. She started believing something good was about to happen.

Suddenly there were three people in the house who had great attitudes, excited about the possibilities. I was the only one with a poor attitude. But not for long. Spending time with them, I began feeling better as their feelings rubbed off.

I began believing in myself again. I got right back into my writing. I was back on purpose, inspired by the kid's dreams. Ninety days later, the manuscript was done! As they say, the rest is history!

Excite Yourself *Every Day*

How are you feeling today? If you feel great, wonderful. But if the feeling you have about the rest of the day makes you want to crawl back into bed, here's a question for you: Why would you want to feel like that? What's the point?

As you scratch your head wondering how I could ask questions like that when I don't really know all the trouble in your life, relax. Everyone has challenges, no matter how carefree they may look! You're in the boat with the rest of us. The great news is *you* choose to feel the way you do by your thinking. Feelings stem from our thoughts and perceptions. Now don't get me wrong; if you have a negative gut feeling about someone or something, that could be a reason for caution.

No one can make you feel any particular way. They may try to influence you and might hit a soft spot, but your reaction or even lack of self-control is totally up to you. They can say or do whatever, but it's your choice as to how you respond. This sure beats reacting inappropriately and hurting a relationship. Be conscientious. Take some time to sort it out rather than saying the first thing that pops into your head. For example, you could say, "I'll let you know later. I need to think it over." The choice is yours—a result of your thinking.

If you make an unwise choice, have the humility to apologize and start again. We all make mistakes. Saying "I'm sorry" can go a long way in fixing a past error, as long as it's sincere.

Not doing so has been the downfall of many, as true success is built on positive relationships.

Consider this. The instant you woke up, you probably thought about getting out of bed and what to do about breakfast. As your mind became clearer, you began thinking about what you had to do that day. You thought about what might work and what might not. Then, all of a sudden—WHAM!

You're thinking about what went wrong yesterday. Things didn't quite work out the way you expected. The next thing you knew, you were behind schedule with a deadline coming up fast. Stress levels rose as you scrambled. The more you rushed, the more things went wrong. It just wasn't your day.

But wait! That was yesterday. You survived. Why would you want to relive it? You may still have to handle some of yesterday's challenges, but nothing says you have to do it by reliving the pain and suffering.

Why not start by being excited about solving these issues, once and for all, preventing their future occurrence? Know that you're the one who can resolve these situations—alone or with help—and you and others will be better off. Giving yesterday's problems a foothold on today is a formula for failure. Eradicate them. You have a brand new day in front of you, filled with possibilities. Use it well. Make it count!

Remember your first day at something new? Recall the nervous excitement? Think back. Remember what made you excited enough to take the chance in the first place? Then start asking some honest questions: "How did I feel?"; "What was my objective?"; "What have I let stand in the way of making it work the way I thought it would?"

When you discard the mental clutter, you'll discover what originally excited you is still there, maybe deeply buried, but still there. Now you can begin again where you first began, only with more wisdom and understanding, looking forward to the task at hand. Instead of making things worse because you felt the excitement was gone, begin anew and you may actually end up better off than you ever imagined. You've learned something about how you can regain your enthusiasm, about what's important to you—how experiencing peaks and valleys is normal. If there were no valleys, how could there be peaks? You welcome challenges as harbingers of positive change.

Who and What Are You Attracting?

We've all heard the expression, "misery loves company," and you may have experienced more than your fair share of it. Can you recall when you were having one of your old bad-attitude days? Before you knew it, you were surrounded by others who were trying to outdo you in the feel-sorry-for-me department. You'd tell your story of woe, only to have them top it. What and who we attract is a reflection of who and what we are, our beliefs, attitudes, and behaviors.

Imagine you're at a party. You're still thinking about the traffic you went through earlier, and the busy day you had at work. As you enter the room, a small group breaks out into un-controllable laughter. What do you do? You find yourself drawn over to them. Eventually, you begin laughing right along with everyone else, maybe without even knowing what's so funny. You enjoy being around happy people because you're emanating more happiness and joy yourself—and they're en-joying being around a more buoyant you!

When laughter fills a room, isn't it easy to accept that being excited will attract others who are capable of being excited? The same people may even help you complete your task be-cause they want to be a part of whatever you're excited about.

For most people, it's always easier to accept the negative—to commiserate. But you're not like most people. You're a winner and you're excited. You've given up on feeling down. You're either up or you're getting up! You set the example, demonstrating that enthusiasm is essential and contagious.

"One man has enthusiasm for 30 minutes, another for 3 days, but it's the man who has it for 30 years who makes a success of his life."

—EDWARD B. BUTLER

"The wise man does not lay up treasure. The more he gives, the more he has."

—Chinese Proverb

14

Sharing Goals Creates Growth

If you've ever attended a meeting, seminar, or other business event, chances are you've learned about goal setting. Clearly identifying and recording the steps to your objective with a timeline is par for achieving long-term success, yet most people fail to do so. This is often why people give up, letting themselves be distracted by the vicissitudes of life, or giving in to a particular situation. They use a myriad of excuses to justify this, rather than admitting they got off course and then immediately getting back on.

But even those who do set goals often don't do it in a way that helps them achieve those goals. They may think about them and maybe even write them down. Some may even go so far as to review them every now and again. While those are certainly necessary components for goal achievement, they're often missing a key part—telling someone else!

There are many benefits to sharing your goals with others you believe will support you. When you tell them your goals, there's a tendency to be more committed. You work toward success to avoid having to face them and admit you've fallen down on the job. You put yourself on the spot. You now have someone to be accountable to—cheerleader, coach, or mentor—and that's a good strategy.

Unfortunately, most people don't write their goals down, let alone tell others, for they fear having to be accountable to themselves! They feel it's better not to commit to something, even though they want it very much. That way they'll never be disappointed. But what they don't realize is the biggest disappointment of all comes in not going for it which, of course, makes it impossible to ever get it! They get a temporary rest by taking themselves off the hook and not going for it. Do they think that what they want is somehow going to magically drop out of the sky someday, and fall right into their laps? I don't think so. It's been proven time and time again that someday becomes a new word called never!

If their desire is true and they're totally sincere, it will come back to haunt them throughout their life. There won't be any long-term reprieve! They may think keeping the desire a secret helps them save face, but they then get to live with disappointment and regret. They succumb to no—right from the get go. This is the main reason for *not* attaining most desires! People are actually telling themselves no before they give themselves a chance for yes and the success it brings.

These people don't want to have to look themselves in a mirror. They don't want others coming up to them constantly asking how they're progressing. Especially if (when!) it isn't going well. They don't want anyone laughing at them. Let them laugh! If they were committed to their goal and took the time to let others know, that fear of being accountable just might be the incentive they need to keep going. It may seem impossible or require a lot of effort, especially at first, but then all worthy aspirations are and do.

Having people who will be reminding you of your goals is a powerful way of keeping them in front of you. Having people who can help you refocus your energy to get the job done is actually something to welcome rather than fear. Telling others is a sign of commitment, as long as it's not empty talk and it's followed by action.

Sharing your goals with others, especially those who have done or know how to do what you're wanting to do, opens up the possibility that these people will help you achieve them. Letting such people know what you want and why, and that you're looking for advice and assistance, often opens the door for others to come into your life and help. If they're in the know themselves, they'll understand that by helping you they enhance their own success. Just the feel-good of doing it can be a big plus for them. The more you go along on your path with a generous heart and spirit, the more you'll realize this.

Oh, and one more thing. Don't share your goals with anyone you believe would be negative toward them. Unfortunately some people get jealous. For your own well-being, just forgive them and avoid burning any bridges you may want to cross later. These folks are often unaware of how detrimental it is to be envious and would be far better off following their own path.

"All things are difficult before they are easy."
—JOHN NORLEY

Success Shouldn't Be Silent

Another great reason for sharing your goals is being able to share in the joy of accomplishment. If you keep your dreams a secret and achieve them, who, other than you, can appreciate the significance of what you've accomplished? By letting others know, you'll find some rooting for you. The appreciative souls who have grown through no and succeeded, may smile and send encouraging thoughts and ideas your way. They understand what it takes to get there.

Now think of a football game. When you're there cheering for a team, it's no secret you want them to win. When they do, isn't it exciting? Of course it is, even though you may have never played the game. You've never scored a touchdown, or blocked, or tackled anyone, yet you were able to share in the joy of victory. It's the same with sharing goals. Those who are aware can get excited and cheer you on, as you press on and enjoy the process of accomplishing what you've set out to do.

When you were in school and earned a great grade on a test or report card, did you keep it a secret? Not likely. You alone did the work to get the grade, yet several people may have been as excited as you were. It gave them joy to see you excel.

Recognize others for their accomplishments. Show appreciation. People going the extra mile need and deserve it. Recognize those who helped you, as no one does it alone. Surveys have shown that recognition ranks higher than money when it comes to reasons why people keep working a particular job. Job satisfaction is enhanced by recognition for good performance.

> *"Who is the happiest? Those who value the merits of others and in their pleasure take joy even as though it were their own."*
>
> —GOETHE

Wouldn't it be nice to have others encouraging you or offering to help you get to where you want to go? The only way that can happen is if you're willing to take a chance and share your dreams and goals, especially with people who can cheer you on. Let them know why you're doing what you're doing; again, tell only those you believe would support you. Don't ask for trouble by sharing your desires with people you know think negatively.

Sharing aspirations with family members who will support you can help justify your need to work more. Overtime, extra hours on a project, or time invested in building an enterprise outside your job affects more than just you. People close to you are more likely to be cooperative when they realize the additional effort might mean a promotion, a raise, an increase in business, or other reward that can be enjoyed by all. If they can participate at some level, and also go after something personally important, all the better. But don't count on that for your success. You just keep doggedly going. After all, you're the one with the dream or objective. Whoever has the strongest dream in any area needs to take the lead. Don't expect others to do it for you!

Instead of people complaining about your time away from them, chances are they'll be more understanding. Remember, if people want to be around you more, you can fix that: Give them something to do with you as you pursue your passion. It's really wonderful when people like to associate more with you! Encourage them to not let you make excuses and cheer you on when they know you're tired. That can help keep you striving toward your goals, rather than giving up. Tell yourself failure is not an option, regardless of how many challenges and noes may come your way.

"Make no little plans; they have no magic to stir anyone's blood. Make big plans, aim high in hope and work."
—Daniel H. Burnham

15

So Why Isn't Everyone Doing Whatever It Takes to Be More Successful?

We get what we consistently put our attention on—pure and simple. Thoughts we carry around in our mind can be glimpses of the future or perhaps a review of where we are today. They can be a reflection of our past thoughts and actions, and result in our focusing on making each day a building block to a brighter future. But they could also be negative thoughts that hold us back. So how are these thoughts determined? How much new input are we giving ourselves—through friends, other people, books, the media, the Internet, experiences, growth?

Our thoughts are often triggered by the questions we ask ourselves, challenging our mind to come up with answers. But if we're only rehashing old ideas that have led to results we're not pleased with, we're on the same worn out path. Our mind leads us to believe the answers we have are the right ones, regardless of the truth. The mind can justify anything that leads to taking a long journey to nowhere. For many, this means habitually thinking and doing the same things over and over again, even if we don't like the consequences. Closed minds lock in perilous thinking, whereas open minds allow truths to come in and resonate.

It's no wonder so many people continue doing the same things. They wake up every day as if they were robots, traveling through the day without much in the way of new thoughts or ideas. They use coffee to get them going, have morning chaos with the kids, and dash to a job they aren't particularly thrilled about. They focus mainly on surviving, and create rather than eradicate debt. Full of frustration and worry, and virtually devoid of conscious purpose and meaning, they run the kids around, scarfing down fast food only to return to the security of home. Next morning the process starts all over again for more of the same.

What's the Point?

But what if they would pause for a few seconds and ask themselves: "What's the point? What's the point of my doing this? What's the point of putting myself through the drudgery of this day-to-day routine only to do it all over again tomorrow? What's the point?"

People often ask these questions but only in a complaining, rhetorical sort of way, internally or to others. Unfortunately, most never ask the next question of themselves, "What can I do about it, once and for all?" They continue to stay stuck, rather than proactively doing something to change the situation they're in. They fail to take their dilemma seriously enough, figuring it'll somehow go away on its own. Rather than taking stock of the condition their lives are in, they essentially run away from it through busyness and whiling away the precious time they could be utilizing to improve things. They're so preoccupied with the treadmill of their lives that they're afraid to reveal their honest thoughts and feelings.

Now let's begin untangling the mess by looking at the possibility of getting some simple yet important answers to the three-word question: "What's the point?" First start with yourself to see where you are regarding all this. Tomorrow, when you wake up, go to the mirror, look into your eyes and ask, "What's the point?" Relax, be still, and the answers will start coming. You'll probably get some basic answers, but maybe something profound will surface.

You might say, "I do this because I'm responsible for the well-being of my family. I chose to live in this neighborhood so we could send our children to a particular school. The skills I've learned are critical to my job or business. Other people are counting on me." And so on....

None of these answers shake the foundation of your being. But, now that you know them, how do you feel about your choice of work? How about your personal life? Feeling a strong love for your family and wanting to provide for them, is a strong driving force. You're watching your children grow in a positive direction because of the sacrifices you've been making on their behalf. You are now motivated to do even better at your job or business so you can reach your financial goals more expeditiously. Your true friends encourage you to excel so you can continue working more with people you know, care about, and trust, as well as other fine people you're attracting and surrounding yourself with.

Now, imagine if other more profound answers start creeping in. Suppose, instead of focusing merely on surviving or maintaining, as you may have been doing, you see a promotion or other income-boosting possibility on the horizon. You ask yourself the same question again: "What's the point?" You envision what a positive change could do for you, your family, friends, and perhaps even your co-workers, associates, or other businesses. With a fresh new perspective, how would you approach what you're now doing?

Might you have a distinctly different outlook from what you have now? Would you like to have more hope and excitement? Do you want to keep doing what you're doing or transition into something else? Could a move be in order?

> *"Unless you endeavor to do something beyond what you have already mastered, you will never grow."*
>
> —RALPH WALDO EMERSON

What's Beyond Your Most Daring Dreams?

People often hesitate to share their dreams, but usually not because they don't *have* dreams or aspirations. More often than not, it's to avoid the disappointment of not achieving them. They might put someone else down who already has what they want. They don't quite believe enough in themselves that they can do it too. When they reached for something better, some were beaten down by ill-advised people or those they mistakenly thought cared about them. Others were told not to get their hopes up, in order to avoid disappointment. Still others were advised to always play it safe, which only developed into a hum-drum life full of regret.

Suppose you want more than just survival or maintaining the status quo. You'd like to succeed beyond your most daring dreams. What's the one thing you absolutely must have? *Daring Dreams!* You can't get to something if you don't know what that something is. If you don't know where the party is, you'll drive right past it, never knowing how good it was.

Having a daring dream or objective firmly in focus will certainly help keep your fires burning. If you don't have a dream or objective, you're working without a real purpose. You're getting nowhere fast, and that's something you can't do happily for very long. You may fool yourself for a little while but, in the long run, you'll feel regret for not having gone for it.

> *"The man who got furthest is generally the one who is willing to do and did. The sure-thing boat never gets far from shore."*
>
> —DALE CARNEGIE

What Naysayers Think About Me and My Dream Is None of *My* Business!

Far too many people are much too concerned about what the rest of the world is saying and doing. They've made it a spectator sport. They're so busy trying to see what everyone else is up to, being an observer of others' successes, that they can't focus on what really needs to be done in their own lives. They're constantly doing or not doing something with a fear-based mentality, not sure where they truly stand or where they're going. They may even rely on the negativity of the media or the Internet, depriving themselves of the life they truly want. They haven't learned that what naysayer's may think about them or their dream is none of their business! Let people think what they will.

Imagine what could be accomplished in just one 24-hour period if everyone in the world concentrated on what *they* needed to be doing—then got it done. Wouldn't that be amazing? People would be a lot happier, that's for sure.

Instead of comparing where we are or what we have to those around us, let's all buckle down and focus on what we really want! Let's go all out, do the work, and enjoy the fruits of our labor. Rather than being concerned that some people might not approve of our decisions, as long as what we're doing is ethically sound, let's stick to our plans. Let's keep moving forward until we accomplish our objective, and then keep going toward a new one.

You've no doubt heard the expression, "Life's too short." While that may be true, we, nonetheless, have all the time there is. We just don't know how much is left for us! Sobering thought, isn't it? The difference is in what we do with the time we have left. Waste it in the court of public opinion and it'll certainly run out before we reach our potential. But when we focus on reaching our objectives, working as hard and as smart as we can to create the outcomes we want, chances are we'll enjoy the time along the way to achieving it.

Once again, the journey is the success. Excitement and success lie in the hunt!

"The quality of a person's life is in direct proportion to his commitment to excellence, regardless of his chosen field of endeavor."

—Vince Lombardi

16

Totally Committed to Excellence

Have you ever shopped in a store looking for something of mediocre quality? Would you trust a doctor who had a reputation of being pretty good? If you were running a company, would you hire applicants who were noted for doing just adequate work?

Could you see yourself driving a new vehicle that has the reputation for working well *most* of the time? Walking into the showroom, you expect every aspect of the new vehicle you're considering to be in perfect working order. You expect the finish to be flawless and shiny, and that the controls, dials, and gauges would all function properly. You automatically assume everything will be in order.

Today, with all the advances in education, technology, and increased competition, high quality is almost a given. It is mass produced. Offering excellence is a prerequisite for being considered a viable player. Anything less and you don't even get to play the game or, at best, you're playing on an average field or for a short period of time. If we honestly expect to win at whatever we're doing, we need to be totally committed to excellence. We need to put forth our own level of excellence—to give our goals what is required.

Whenever we get involved in something new, or are considered for a task or position, excellence needs to be a foregone conclusion—in our performance and whatever we're offering, but especially in the relationships we're building along the way. If we treat others shoddily or try to manipulate or ramrod over them in our quest to succeed, we are in for a rocky road that leads to a dead end.

Some have thoughts on how to get something done as quickly as possible, regardless of how it's done or who may be hurt in the process. Others look for ways to do things with less effort, even if the results are abominable; they simply don't care. Still others spend a great deal of time looking for ways *not* to do much of anything, to just skate, trying to maintain the status quo.

This book is not about judgment—it's about thought stimulation, suggestions, and taking action. Have you ever noticed that it often takes little more time, attention, or effort to produce excellence rather than mediocrity? Have you observed that the difference in the outcomes can be incredible? Horse races are often won by a nose! If only more people would take that to heart.

What if you committed to thirty days of excellence? You give every task or challenge a 100 percent effort to produce and complete them all with as little error as possible. Your only focus is on doing a great job, whether you're building something, writing a report, making a presentation, coaching a youth group, or applying yourself to some other endeavor.

First of all, you start each day looking your best. You get to work or to your assignment mentally sharp, on time, and ready to go. You're a do-it-now person. You have no other thoughts in mind except the completion of the task. Most importantly, you welcome the challenge of being selected or having the opportunity to demonstrate what you've got. What could be the possible outcomes? Can you think of anything negative? I don't think so!

Be a Contrarian—*Do the Opposite of What Everybody Else Is Doing!*

"Don't get your hopes up." "Be satisfied with what you have." "Don't rock the boat." "You can't fight city hall." Ever hear anything like that? These sayings are as old as dinosaurs.

But what if you took each of these success-robbing clichés and did exactly the opposite? Suppose you really got your hopes up—for everything in life? Suppose you set your sights way above and beyond where you are now? Suppose you're finally willing and, therefore, going to do whatever it takes, even if it rocks the boat, toward achieving those high aspirations?

We all need to be grateful for what we have. It's part of being happy. That's a given. But there's nothing wrong with some dissatisfaction, either, provided one is going to use it to propel themselves to do something about it. It's essential for change. Yes. Be thankful for what you have, health, family, home, work, and such, for sure. But, it's perfectly fine and admirable to believe there's more for you in this life. As long as you're willing to become more than you are at the moment, and consistently take action to do so, you can do it. Keep in mind the tremendous hurdles overcome by those who have blazed the path before you.

> "Progress always involves risk; you can't steal second base with one foot on first."
>
> —FREDERICK WILCOX

Fight for what you know is right, even if it's against city hall, so to speak. Others will likely join you once they sense your passion and the steadfastness you exhibit toward your worthy goal. Just because many people believe something and have agendas reflecting that, doesn't necessarily make it the right thing to do. You've undoubtedly observed that countless times. Turn the tables if it's for the ultimate good of all.

Your actions need to always be accelerating in excellence, reflective of your ever-improving efforts—benefiting others as well as yourself. Carefully consider how you do things. Interact with people in the kindest, most authentic, forthright, and effective way. This will help those around you in the long-run, even if they don't now realize or appreciate it. It also helps get and keep you at a consistently higher level of performance. When someone becomes self-centered about something, the quality of their efforts diminishes. They never really feel good about it, although they may put on a good front. Taking our eyes off of ourselves and putting them onto others is key. Pushing ahead, our self-concern fades into the background.

Are You Merely Going Along for the Ride, or *Are You In Control and Really Going Somewhere?*

Making a commitment, in and of itself, is not difficult; the challenge is in keeping it. If we don't keep our commitments to our goals, how can we expect to be successful? Keep the objective firmly fixed in your mind. Know where you want to go and why it's important for you to get there. Remind yourself of it every day. Post it on your computer screensaver.

Put up pictures and affirmative statements in your home, work area, vehicle, mirror, and other areas you see often. This will help you remember to keep your commitment. It's what happens as we travel that can distract us from our destination—but only for as long as we let it. Like stopping for gas or to take care of an emergency, we get right back on the road and follow our chosen path.

Keep your objectives in focus and you'll reduce the obstacles, challenges, and noes encountered along the way to mere speed bumps, brief delays, or detours. You'll be aware of them as you go, but you won't let them force you to cancel the trip. Keep the ups and downs in that positive, forward-moving perspective. Continue on the most direct path available. Don't look for ways to avoid or sidestep. Just power through the noes that threaten to delay or stop your journey.

There are times when a failing effort or other setback can temporarily alter your focus. When that happens, deal with it head-on—changing whatever needs to be changed, attitude- or action-wise. This will reduce or eliminate the likelihood of that situation happening again. Avoiding its reoccurrence is the best, most energy- and time-efficient precaution. After you've dealt with the issue, be sure to refocus and get right back on the road to your goal. Otherwise, the potential for getting lost or even forgetting the purpose of the trip can interfere with your quest.

One way to notice if you've lost focus is if you start feeling undue stress and then question the value of proceeding. Be careful here, or you could set yourself up to receive a no from yourself! Take a step back and revisit the reason why you're doing what you're doing. Are you just letting yourself get bogged down by a never-win frame of mind? Are you letting naysayers get you down? Exactly what is it that you need to go on? Encouragement? Who can help you in some way? Associate with winners who are also in the achievement game, not those on the sidelines telling you no.

> *"The greatest good you can do for another is not just to share your riches, but to reveal to him his own."*
> —BENJAMIN DISRAELI

Can you still see what you're after? If not, chances are, you're focusing on either avoiding a situation you don't want to face, or doing it with deflective action or inaction. You may be stuck expending too much cautionary effort in preventing a repeat of what just occurred. Maybe it was a no. We all get them so we might as well accept that and keep moving. If we're not getting any noes, we're not doing much. So get as many noes as you can!

If you missed the mark, spend a few quiet moments reconfiguring your goals. When all is said and done, where do you want to be by a particular date? Once you've accomplished this, you'll find the challenge you were dwelling on may not even need dealing with. You may just need to put blinders on, like a champion racehorse, and blow by the obstacles and nay-sayers. Prove them wrong and win by a nose!

Dr. Stephen Covey said, "Begin with the end in mind." Maintain eagle-eye sight of whom and what you're working for and why, and the obstacles and setbacks along the way will generally be small and temporary. You may not even see them! What you focus on increases its presence. Make sure it's your objective!

Being totally committed to excellence gives you the strength to stay on target, and the power to keep anything that comes along from overshadowing it. Striving for excellence is an energy booster. It gives you the confidence to know that, as long as you remain true to your goals, steadfast in your efforts, there's no obstacle big enough to keep you from your reward.

Being totally committed to excellence in all matters entrusted to your care is a quintessential quality of success. Working at it until excellence becomes a habit reinforces you to build on its solid foundation. You'll attract excellent people who will respect you and work with you so that everyone can reach their objectives. You'll find yourself living an excellence-driven life, enjoying the fellowship of excellence-driven people.

"The spirit, the will to win, and the will to excel are the things that endure. These qualities are so much more important than the events that occur."

—VINCE LOMBARDI

17

Hall of Fame Habits

Could you talk about your children all day long? I could. There are so many things they do and have done that I feel good about. While they have had the opportunity to learn many valuable life lessons because of my career, the best lessons didn't come from me.

My son was having difficulty with a sport he was participating in. Driving home from an event one night, he went on and on about how little talent he had, that he'd never be good enough. Down on himself, not having any fun, his self-doubt grew as he kept beating himself up. His prognostications would've surely set him up for failure or the lack of desire to even try.

In times like these you hope the other person will listen as you strive to help them get past a no-win-for-anybody mood or situation. First I just sat, tuned in to his downward discourse, letting him fully express his feelings, waiting patiently for an answer to come as how best to support him.

Driving on, we started listening to a basketball game on the radio. The most popular player back then was Michael Jordan. My son adored him. Serendipitously enough, they were just about to interview him. I couldn't have planned or paid for anything more timely or profound.

The reporter stated that when he watched Michael during the game all he saw was joy; it looked as though he was having great fun. The reporter went on to say that Michael's attitude made him really stand out because all the other players looked disgruntled and mean, as if they were fighting a war, out to get the guys on the other team. But Michael shared a spirit of friendly competition.

There was a pause and, since we were stopped at a traffic light, I glanced over at my son, listening intently. Michael said something like: "When I practice, I practice as if it were a war. This way, I'm so prepared that when I get to the game I just enjoy playing my level best. Many other players play at practice and consequently have to fight a war during the game."

I never said a word about that interview to my son. He never complained about his ability again.

Greatness Doesn't Just Happen—*It's Earned!*

Whether it's athletics, business, entertainment, the arts, science, or whatever passion you may have, there are people you respect as the greatest at what they do. I, too, have heroes in different arenas who I look to as examples of greatness. But while I admire their accomplishments and enjoy their performances as much as others, I *learn* from them. My perceptiveness goes beyond what much of the rest of the world sees.

Get behind the end result and all that may glitter on the surface, and you can discover the effort it took to get there. You'll learn about a work ethic seldom duplicated by others in that field. You'll see a rarely matched dedication to reaching for excellence in everything they do. For example, an artist may make an initial rough sketch of a painting. I've seen some of those rough sketches.

I wish I could even come close to that in my *finest* artistic endeavors. They sketch such a great practice picture that when the time comes for the creation of the final work, the details just fall into place. The only thing added is a deeper reflection of the passion they have for what they're doing.

Persistence is required in creating greatness. One cannot stand above the crowd and expect to be recognized as great simply by saying it's so. You need to be the real deal—not just present a facade, image, or fabrication based on appearances. Humility is a central characteristic in greatness.

Many who have reached an esteemed level did so not because they were brilliant. They simply wouldn't give up—even when no one recognized their work until it had been around for years, decades, or even beyond death. They didn't do it for glory. They just did what was inside them to do in following their dream. Their passion drove them to excel, enabling them to contribute to the world. Risk avoidance was not an option. They realized it would actually be riskier not to take a risk!

> *"The price of greatness is responsibility."*
> —WINSTON CHURCHILL

Another consistency I've observed in those who have achieved high levels of accomplishment is the determination to constantly be learning more about their craft. They're always putting that knowledge into practice, pushing forward. Many people curiously ask how to do something, but only a few take the next step—taking the answer and running with it, putting it into action. It's the action that really counts—the continuous movement toward the goal. Without it, a very ordinary life ensues. With a change of mind and heart, and essential fine-tunes, your continuous focused action is most important in creating the habits necessary for long-term success.

Instant Is for Pudding—*Keep Cooking*

The Baseball Hall of Fame is filled with exhibits of special moments in the history of the sport. But its primary function is to pay tribute to the greatest players. If you have the opportunity to visit, even if you're not a fan of the game, you'll see one of the most important ingredients for greatness.

Baseball is filled with players who can hit the ball further, throw it harder and, perhaps, even play the game better, now and again, than many of the members enshrined in the Hall of Fame. Yet, many of them never get nominated. Why?

Those who've been nominated and inducted were honored because their extraordinary level of play was not just in one great game, one great season, or even a handful of years. Those in the Hall of Fame are there because their level of excellence was consistent over a lifetime of seasons. They played the game at the highest level, not just when they felt like it or when it was necessary, but over the entire span of their career. For them, every game counted. Every game got nothing less than wholehearted contribution. Hall of Fame habits rule their lives. Spurts of momentary heroic effort aren't good enough.

Bestselling authors seldom achieve that level with their first book. They could get on a bestseller list with their first published effort, but many times one or more of their previous manuscripts are sent to the recycling bin or remain on an editor's rejection pile because they weren't good enough. Those authors, instead of looking at themselves as failures, looked at what they finished simply as practice—less than what they're ultimately capable of. More importantly, they continued writing, constantly improving, completing one book, moving on to the next. Keeping their eyes fixed on the prize, they eventually produced something of significance.

The goal to become published is often missed because writers start paying attention to the individual answers they get along the way, allowing discouragement to set in. Many quit after only a few noes from a handful of selected publishers. The great authors are those who never gave up on the one person central to their achieving greatness—themselves. They look at the person in the mirror every day and ask, "What action will I take today to move closer to the goal?"

The Shortcut to Greatness

Fad diets, get-rich-quick schemes, and the like are all very popular. Our society wants it all and they want it now. So since everyone's looking for a shortcut, here it is! Do whatever it takes to go and grow through the noes so you can get to the yeses that will shape your life and lead to greatness.

Great success is possible—provided your commitment is rock solid. Do things the average person won't. Observe where the crowd is headed and, instead, follow your own path. Always be growing yourself, driving toward your objective.

Find someone who's at or above the level of greatness or success you've decided to attain. Ask, read about, and watch them present, in person or on audio or video, listening carefully to what they say. Discover what they did to get there, why they did it, and how they stayed on top of their game. Commit to getting a tighter grip on your own objective, going at it harder and staying at it longer than they did. Do whatever it takes to reach beyond the goal they reached. Why not do even better than they did? Push yourself. See how far you can go.

Work harder than you've ever worked before. This is a hallmark of those at the top! Winners in the making watch others succeed and then endeavor to surpass them by moving their own bar of excellence even higher. As time passes, the new achievers seem to rise up out of nowhere. Look at all the hard work the person you admire did and do more.

Those who put themselves down only fall back, thinking they're satisfied with where they are, knowing full well they're just being lazy. The committed reject the status quo, realizing greatness is just over the horizon. They use disgruntlement to motivate themselves to excel.

Take it one day at a time. It doesn't matter how long it will take or how hard it may be to get there. Never let any difficulty stop you. Keep working at it with the tenacity of a Hall of Famer. Make it a habit and you'll be on top of your game. Do it all your life and you may find yourself inducted into a Hall of Fame.

"Success is to be measured not so much by the position one has reached in life as by the obstacles he has overcome while endeavoring to succeed."

—BOOKER T. WASHINGTON

18

Reaching Success on Your Own Terms

A spiring leaders take full advantage of learning from others. They understand that being humble, teachable, and open-minded are fundamental to being a strong leader. They even learn from people apparently not worthy of emulation, as they often show us what *not* to do! A trusted mentor can be one of your greatest allies in helping you determine what's best for you in moving forward. Knowing you, your situation, and aspirations, they can assist with prioritizing, recommending time lines, and showing you what to do.

A lot of people, though, are virtually puppets, moving in response to the strings others pull, not paying attention to their own inner compass. This is one of the main reasons they're dissatisfied with their lot in life. Many are stressed out, having relinquished their destinies to other's agendas. They're so used to having decisions made for them—from parents, to bosses, to so-called friends, and any others who influence them, including the media and the Internet. Many people can't seem to figure

out why they're unhappy or how to change things. They roboti-
cally whir on in their daily activities, oblivious to what being
discontent is doing to themselves and others. Sadly, they keep
doing what others say they should do.

While I'm all for seeking advice and learning from those
with more knowledge and experience, *you* need to be the one
who decides what success is for you. If not, the cost could be
devastating, emotionally as well as financially. Consider this
example of dollars and cents.

Let's say you sell cars for a living, earning an average of
$300 for each one you sell. That's fine, but there's a problem;
you're in the habit of letting others decide your success.

You live in an above-average neighborhood and have a
higher-than-average mortgage. Like many others, you have a
poor debt/income ratio and you made a minimum down pay-
ment, giving you a higher interest rate. You send your kids to
private school because that's what people in the neighborhood
do. You look good but you're broke. To maintain all the trap-
pings, you need to earn $6,000 a month. So you grab your
lunch and head off to work, having figured out how many cars
you need to sell.

That morning, after fighting gridlock, you're rushing in the
door to pour a quick cup of coffee before attending your
monthly sales meeting. Here, the harried manager reports how
many cars each of his salespeople needs to sell in order for the
dealership to be successful. When he comes to you, looking
down at his spreadsheet, not even glancing up, he gruffly an-
nounces you're responsible for selling 15 cars—finalizing it
with a loud clearing of his raspy throat.

What if you reach that goal? Are you successful? According to your boss, who barely notices you, and probably many
others at the dealership, you are. Why? The boss is paid to decide! But here's the problem. At $300 commission a car, you
would earn only $4,500 a month. You'll succeed at your job.
But, by measuring up to your manager's standards, who never
consults with you, you'll fail on the home front. You're $1,500

short! You really need to sell 20 cars this month just to survive at your current standard of living. This, of course, doesn't include any unexpected expenses and spending money to enjoy, not to mention putting furniture in the empty rooms of your big new house.

Can you understand how stress and dissatisfaction could come into play? How the head can pound and stomach churn because you've let someone else you wouldn't choose as a friend, let alone a mentor, decide how your financial picture should be painted? There's nothing wrong with any of the goals and rewards mentioned here. They can all be attained, even under current circumstances. But unless you're stretching to reach them, what's the point of having them? You'll fall short of what you really want to accomplish, and stay on the losing end of things.

The next time you're considering following someone else's plan, someone who doesn't have your best interests at heart, consider this: If you reach *their* objective for you, are you short in meeting your own? If so, I'd wonder if they'd mind paying *your* bills!

Increased Productivity Can Lead to *a Better Life*

Let's look at another example, similar in many ways, but changing the scenario a bit. Suppose you're living in only an average neighborhood so your expenses are manageable, but the kids go to a poorly rated public school. What happens if you move *and* send the kids to a private school? Wouldn't you be happier choosing when *you* want to make these things happen? You'd rather not rely on someone else's agenda and schedule. You want more control of your life.

Let's start at work first.

You go to your sales meeting and the boss says your number is 15 cars. At $4,500 a month, you figure it'll take about two years to save enough of a down payment to afford the type of house you'd like, for which the payments are somewhat reasonable. You realize that if you want the house even faster, selling one extra car a month could make it happen six months sooner. But to hedge your bets, just in case some unforeseen expense arises, you up your goal to two extra cars a month.

Or, let's say you decide that your kids' educations are more important than a bigger house, and that a nearby private school will do the trick. To make this transition, you need to sell three extra cars a month to get rolling—gearing up to pay tuition first—deferring your house purchase six more months.

Whatever way *might* work for you, here's what the results mean: In both scenarios, you end up with the house and your children get a private education.

So what's the difference?

Doing it the first way, you're house poor—financially over-burdened—like most people who nervously live on the brink of financial disaster. Some in upscale neighborhoods are so strung out financially that they can't even afford draperies let alone essential furniture to fill the rooms of their mini-mansions. Like many today, the bank may have to foreclose if you aren't in good enough fiscal shape to withstand one of life's little sur-prises. You are owned by your employer, who may use your good nature to take unfair advantage of you. They may know full well you're on the financial edge and wouldn't mind your staying there, giving them more control over you.

In-between these two examples, you'd need to downsize back to average living quarters if you're living beyond your means. If you don't, you may lose a wad on the facade of wealth you've shakily built, especially if it's a down real estate market. But imagine how much you'd continue to lose if you kept practicing the same old financially irresponsible habit? You'll resent everything about the house, your kid's education and, ultimately, the job that seems to be holding you hostage.

If you waited just a little while longer, while pepping up your sales, you could have both the house and the educational costs covered—with a lot less stress. Your job, with your more meaningful focus would be providing for your needs, giving you more satisfaction.

If you don't like what you're doing, money won't be of much help, causing your sales to plummet. After all, who wants to buy from a miserable salesperson? Your efforts, one way or the other, will produce certain results. Taking charge of your goals enhances your ability to provide, rather than acquiescing to an outside force because you believe you have to. This could be the strongest motivator you've ever had, and a catalyst to let go of the anchor hanging around your neck.

You made the decision that having those things would represent a level of success *you* want to achieve. No one else is pulling your strings. You created a plan to achieve your goals and did the work to earn them. What a great outcome!

"Genius is the ability to hold one's vision steady until it becomes reality."

—BENJAMIN FRANKLIN

Not Choosing Is Also a Choice!

You're exactly where you've chosen to be—proactively or by acquiescing—for better or for worse. Stressed out? Broke? Dissatisfied? It's all you, yesiree, whether you like it or not. You chose to be right where you are. There's no one to blame but yourself. "What?" you demand. You're probably thinking there's no way you'd ever choose to have any of those challenging situations in your life. Really?

What decisions in life have you made to *prevent* those things from happening? In many cases, those negative results are caused by a decision to defer to others who decide your destiny—to set your bar. Are you a passive recipient of others' dictates in the workplace? Or are you taking appropriate charge of your destiny like winners do? Are you focused on and striving for the life you've always wanted? Or are you like a rubber raft bouncing to and fro, at the mercy of the waves made by other people's decisions, unwise examples, or the environment around you?

Is there some other place you'd rather be? Something you'd like to have, maybe more time with your family or traveling more? Something you'd like to be? Some knowledge you'd like to acquire? There's only one solution: Determine and do whatever it takes to make whatever you want to happen. No one else is going to do it for you—maybe *with* you, when you're enthusiastic and engaging—but not *for* you. Do you have enough respect for yourself and your family, and the one life you've been given, to do that? Well, for crying out loud, show the world what's in you! If you believe people underestimate you, it's because you're not showing them or yourself!

When you work to make things happen, life becomes richer and more meaningful. Sure you'll have other challenges, more noes! So what? Great. You're going to have challenges anyway, so why not get moving and get on with it, and make some really wonderful things happen? Why not have "This person made his dreams come true," on your tombstone? And what about "This person cared about others and made a difference." Wouldn't that be special? Wouldn't it be better than "Same old, same old is the way she lived, just trudging along"?

Otherwise, why bother? If you are completely satisfied with where you are, go ahead and keep doing what you're doing. But I don't believe it! I don't believe you're completely satisfied, or you wouldn't be reading this book. I'm not completely satisfied—I have *much* more to do. How about you? Come on now! We all do. We just don't know how much time we have left to do it. We all need to keep moving rather than wimping out like the average person. As long as we're alive, we need to be doing *our own* thing.

Simply letting things happen puts someone else in control of your future and makes your life poorer. Unless you have a specific plan that you're implementing, your life and everything you work for will be in the hands of someone else.

Solidly commit to achieving the outcomes you want, taking one step then another. As you gather momentum your project will take on a life of its own. It'll be easier to stay on track, developing the knowledge, habits, and skills necessary to successfully complete the next phase of the journey. If someone else is determining your future, it's easy to come up with excuses why you're not there; why you're not where you want to be; why you're not doing anything about your unhappiness. You'll just blame it on them. You say they're the ones holding you back. How fruitless! *They* won't make you successful—I guarantee it! You need to create your own success. Both the I-never-get-yes and the I'm-determined-to-get-yes paths are habit forming. Which path and habit will you choose?

If you honestly want more success, clearly choose yes by not being afraid of no. Remember, noes strengthen you for the possibilities yeses bring. That knowledge will serve you well, keeping you going, when things don't quite go according to how you thought they would.

Detours and noes will always be encountered, and that's okay! But always aim for yes and the destination. Your dedication and consistent drive to achieve it will create the habits necessary to make succeeding second nature. You'll blast through the obstacles and get really good at it!

We've all noticed people who seem to succeed at everything they do. While that's probably not the case, these individuals, nevertheless, *have* developed habits of excellence. They've developed a persistence that defies defeat in the face of no. It, along with great growth and strong faith, helps them get all the press-on power boosts they need.

Your choice to read this book is one essential step, a main ingredient toward forming permanent success habits. Developing yourself personally and professionally is critical to building confidence and belief in yourself. Keep going when others around you are protesting and questioning your decisions and actions. Reach success on your own terms, not someone else's.

"Nothing splendid has ever been achieved except by those who dared believe that something inside of them was superior to circumstance."

—BRUCE BARTON

19

Unique—It's What Makes You, You

How could anyone expect success without taking the initiative? Sure, others may buy in to what they're doing but no one is going to do it for them.

You might be shocked at how many are waiting for something extraordinary to happen to turn the tide! But the truth is, whoever has the strongest desire to accomplish something is the one who must take the lead in making it happen.

For example, if one spouse wants new flooring in the house more than the other, who needs to push for it? The one with the strongest desire. This is certainly obvious, but how many of us apply this principle to success?

For greater success, lead others who could also benefit from what you're offering or doing. Set the course of your life to have maximum significance and meet challenges head on, defeating them instead of letting them defeat you. Enjoy the satisfaction that comes from the victory of overcoming hurdles that threaten to take you off course.

You'll get stronger and more and more confident, yet remain humble, knowing you couldn't have done it alone. Recognize the many variables that go into the mix of success—the materials, products, services, tools, transportation, coordination of people and events, leadership, schedules, camaraderie with peers, the list goes on. Keen, broad-minded, perceptive observation reveals the interwoven nature of what's behind the scenes.

Once you have a way of achieving success, keep at it—repeating the basics over and over. You'll become really good at it, like those you admire. We all must do the basics—losing site of them is fatal to our success, no matter what we're doing. Learn your craft and keep up with the changes.

Promote, promote, promote. Call, call, call. Develop those key relationships. Focus on others. What can *you* do for *them*? As a task is completed or a goal achieved, use the ingredients you incorporated to realize it again in bigger ways, maximizing the difference you're making. This can support doing what you love more often as you transition into it.

While we all use our own methods and techniques in certain situations, core principles are universally unfailing. Regardless of circumstances, conditions, rules, or obstacles, one thing you can count on is that proven principles work. Keep upgrading your own application of them. Always be on the cutting edge with continuous learning and development.

> *"Little minds attain and are subdued by misfortune; but great minds rise above them."*
> —Washington Irving

Keep going and you'll find yourself making breakthrough after breakthrough. Continuously risk no and you'll grow. Remember, it's okay to *feel* like quitting; knowing your character and integrity won't let you! It would only be a disservice to yourself and others. Work with every fiber of your being, giving it your all, and you'll be rewarded with gifts greater than even the accomplishment of your goal. You'll surprise yourself as you discover strengths you didn't even know you had. They'll work for you whenever summoned, enabling you to spread your wings and fly. Their thrust will propel you to new heights, and they can never be taken away from you.

What's *Your* Story?

I've been privileged to travel the world and observe people from all walks of life. I've seen those who've held on to the anonymity of blending in, as well as those who've risked no countless times to reach the yeses that allowed them to stand out. Everyone has a story.

Those who wish to remain as they are have a story as to why they can't do things, and how they're victims of this and that. "Under the circumstances," they'll say in a weak tone. "I don't have time," they'll groan, as if those who achieve have more hours in a day. They give in to no as if it signifies the end of the road rather than the beginning of a great journey. Instead of persevering to get yes, they give up by saying "why bother." They're full of the sadness of what could have been, blaming someone or something else for their plight.

Then there are those who know it's up to them. They pour their heart and soul into it, working with a determination that can only be satisfied with ongoing growth and accomplishment. Their stories have power and punch and are rich with passion and adventure. Others often share their stories, using them to inspire still more.

> *"To dream anything you want to dream. That is the beauty of the human mind. To do anything you want to do. That is the strength of the human will. To trust yourself to test your limits. That is the courage to succeed."*
>
> —BERNARD EDMONDS

We all have setbacks, but they help us stay on top of our game and keep life fun and challenging. Noes are a good thing. Growing through them builds character and skill. Going to great lengths for small gains is part of it, along with the fatigue.

Overcoming bouts of self-doubt, while working without seeing the desired results as quickly as we would have liked, builds character. Hang in there. The prize is waiting for you, right around a corner you have yet to turn.

Putting it all together, you're creating a story to tell. Without challenges, without noes, life is boring at best. You'd have little or nothing to help you grow, little or nothing to share, except the same old same old.

It's great and essential to read, and learn what needs to be done. But no one is successful by just being a book, audio, or seminar junkie, not following it all up with action. When others first hear of your growth and accomplishments, they may be thinking they could never even hope to do what you did. But when they hear your story of overcoming the obstacles you met along the way, they could become tremendously encouraged to venture out more on their own journey. You could become a positive example of how to be, think, and what to do. Maybe you already are. We're all examples of some kind. What kind would you like to be?

If I wouldn't have ventured out on my own, subjecting myself to noes and failings, I wouldn't have accomplished very much. If I hadn't overcome my lack of self-confidence, I'd have nothing to say that could help you. Add to it that I had virtually no income for over a year while I wrote my first book, and that over a hundred publishers turned me down, and it starts to get interesting.

Now throw in the constant hassle my ex-boss gave me about how I would never do this and you can see how success is the greatest revenge! The bottom line is that without having had lots of challenges to overcome and always taking on new ones, I would never have had any books published. My life would have been a ho-hum boring average existence.

Think about it. Weren't the greatest movies you've ever seen and the best books you've ever read filled with stories of highs and lows and overcoming? The more challenges, even tragedies, the better the story. Don't you just love seeing an underdog master him- or herself and the dilemmas, and rise above it all?

Gain mastery by pursuing your own "pie in the sky." Keep pressing on, using your story as you help others. Building on your successes, then sharing them with others, will also keep *you* inspired as you continue your journey in this opportunity called life.

It'll help you realize that yes, you do have staying power in the face of adversity, and you can repeat it again and again, whenever needed. You could also be granted the privilege, as I have, to speak on stage and share what you've gone through and how it has all paid off, even though it may not have felt like it would at the time. You'll see how faces light up when hope is renewed.

No matter what the future may bring, no one can ever take your story away from you. So make it really good as you keep going and growing through the inevitable noes. You'll be richer for it as a human being and set a greater example for others to follow. Whatever it turns out to be, the process is worth it all, and it'll make you feel good knowing you're making a difference in others' lives.

Just a Little More

Being unique doesn't mean everything about you or everything you do has to be original. You'll be quite unique simply by being yourself, while emulating the attitudes and actions of those you admire.

When you follow the example set by successful people who have achieved what you'd like to achieve, your ingenuity will surface. Unfortunately, the majority of people are too busy blending in, trying to escape the experience of life unnoticed. They're copying those who happen to be to their left and to their right, rather than the ones ahead of them. Part of your uniqueness is that you're in the minority—there's only one you and you have a distinct purpose that only you can live out in your own special way.

"The greatest thing a man can do is to make the most of the stuff that has been given him. This is success, and there is no other."

—ORISON SWETT MARDEN

Observe what average people do and commit to doing a little more a little better, and make the most of each moment in doing so. That alone boosts you to above average, helping make you more unique in the scheme of things. As you stay above average, while raising your thinking and behavior, you'll eventually rise up further still. Other achievers will notice and appreciate your efforts. Your respect and credibility will become more evident, even to those who regard you with envy and maybe scorn. They may feel you are a better person than they are, yet not be willing to grow themselves. That's sad. They could join you but, instead, make excuses. Always hold them well in your heart. Know an epiphany or crisis could occur to change their minds, bringing them to their senses.

In the meantime, keep shining. Be a guiding light and you'll be doing the right thing. Continue making your uniqueness stand out as you grow and become more outstanding, raising the bar as you continue.

Do you think you're just average and can't grow? You're not and I'll prove it! Hopefully this goes a long way in helping you on your journey of success. It may not be readily apparent to you but it does put you in the more successful minority.

Get this. The average person buys only one book a year. Appalling, isn't it? Furthermore, they read only one chapter, if that. Reading this far into this book automatically puts you above average! If this is the first book you've purchased this year, get another one in the success genre. Continue growing yourself, rising above the crowd.

Consider that most people aren't happy with their job or work situation. The ideal scenario, of course, is to love what you do and the environment in which you're doing it. If you don't, however, decide that it's only temporary. Know you can handle it for the time being, as long as you're doing it to support someone you love or until you achieve a certain goal. That attitude puts you above average. You may not love your job, but you love the reason you're still doing it.

Your job may require a lot of overtime, and it may be hard work. Perhaps it's enabled you to pay your bills, but you may realize it won't get you where you want to go long-term. If you dislike or hate what you do, look to transition out of it—even if doing it has earned you a lot of money! Would you want your tombstone to read, "He made a lot of money but died a stressed-out, unhappy, unfilled person. He didn't do what was inside of him to do. Sure, he made a lot of money, but he missed the boat. He missed the joy of life"? How sad is that?

Confidently go forward in the direction of your greatest dream. Use the one and only life you have, and the opportunities you've been given, and let your uniqueness shine through.

"Dost thou live life? Then do not squander time, for it is the stuff life is made of."

—BENJAMIN FRANKLIN

20

NOW Is the Only Time You Have to Do Anything!

Several years ago, my son was chosen to play for a baseball team. Even though he had the honor of being the youngest picked, which I told him was a compliment, he was *still* discouraged. The team had finished dead last the summer before. From the moment he received the call, he was almost sorry he had ever tried out.

Fortunately, they had a coach who had a lot more on the ball than your typical baseball coach. He was generous of heart, with an immense make-it-happen perspective—a well grounded giver who knew the value of a get-to-it attitude. To help mentor the team in transforming their down-in-the-dumps, no-win attitude, he did one of the things that works best for engendering team spirit in preteen ballplayers: he bought them all T-shirts with a picture of a baseball field on the front!

Each of the kids grinned ear to ear as they got one. They were so excited, they immediately put them on, forgetting about where the team finished last year. They all dashed out to the field to begin practice, looking like players who were meant to work together to do increasingly better than their best. At that moment, the cloud hiding the sun moved to the left and the whole field seemed to light up like never before. But the genius wasn't just in the new shirts; it was what the coach had printed on the back in big block letters:

"NEXT YEAR IS NOW!"

After a rigorous practice, the kids' sweat glistening, parents smiling, the coach had the team sit down while he explained what the back of the shirt meant. He told them that what happened last year was over. He said what they wanted for the coming season—to win and win big—depended on what they did beginning today, at that very moment. "Next year is now! Let me hear it," he shouted. "Next year is now!" the team shouted back.

Where do *you* want to be in the next twelve months? While writing down your answers is certainly recommended, it's most important to immediately get moving and begin pursuing them. Next year *is* now! What you do today and for the next 365 days largely determines where you'll be. Your decisions and, more importantly, follow-up actions will either bring you closer to your goals or take you further away from them. They'll either lead to victory and rejoicing or losing and regretting. What will it be for you?

Get Over It and *Get On with It!*

No one is really surprised when they finally understand that life isn't always easy—for themselves or anyone else! Most nod in quick agreement when told that obstacles, failed attempts, and noes are coming. But it can be quite different when those occurrences actually happen.

There is often a period of mourning followed by a time of retreat, keeping to oneself, where nothing new is attempted. Then, as is often the case, the quest is either abandoned or put aside, only to be brought up if someone asks, "How are things going with _____?" Then a litany of excuses is used to "explain" why things are no further along than the last time the subject was discussed.

Generally, the conversation fades to something else of little consequence. People may see through the excuses if they're not excuse makers themselves, but might not care enough to help the person get out of his or her own way. They can't risk taking the relationship to the edge. They may not realize that just a little encouragement may be the best gift they can give—that it can make a real difference.

But why *would* someone give up in the first place? Why would they let one or more setbacks, one or more noes, determine their future? Simply because they deal in the past—they dwell on past failures. They have grabbed hold of and believe that history repeats itself. They keep repeating old mistakes and don't make the changes to create the bigger life they say they want.

In order to avoid the possibility of going through the noes again, they cower in fear, avoid planning, and don't do anything toward realizing their goals. They acquiesce, surrendering to their circumstances, focusing on the tiniest of obstacles. They don't look seriously enough at their own stuck thinking and behavioral patterns to understand that this is exactly why history *will* repeat itself. They may have initially made a little progress but then regressed to the same old thoughts and actions, getting the same old results.

But history doesn't just randomly repeat. As long as we learn from what we've created in the past, and modify our thinking and approach, we're unlikely to experience the exasperation of doing the same old things over and over again. It may seem like a reprieve to ignore our role in what happened and not take responsibility for it, but refusing to learn from our errors and move on creates a recurring theme. Unpleasant events that could have been avoided by forging a new direction are still occurring.

Protecting yourself from challenges invites the repetition of failing and no into your life. If, after a setback, no, or failed attempt you decide to seek shelter to avoid disappointment, you'll most surely be even *more* disappointed in the long-run. So take responsibility and just go for it! Failure is guaranteed to those who take a backseat in life. By staying hidden from the possibility of being hurt, we're also hiding from success and the people who could come into our lives and help us succeed. They'll just find others who are game for taking the plunge and will stick to it to reach *their* goals. We end up just looking on, thinking how lucky these folks are.

Once again, the pain we feel when things don't go according to plan—when we get a no—is never pleasant. But that simply doesn't matter. It's just part of the success process. We need to go at it squarely and continue anyway. The quickest way to get over it is not to hide behind it. Instead, face the reality of it, learn from it, and push through it with a new or modified approach. Move vigorously forward, renewing your commitment to continue the journey. As soon as you take the first step of your next attempt, forgiving the past, its negative sting fades away. Your focus happily returns to the possibilities you can achieve through yes. In your mind, dare the world to "Go ahead. Tell me no. You can't hold me down. I'm on the grow! I'll show you."

Today Has Got to Be *the* Day

People are always looking for the sure thing. It's human nature to want everything quick and easy. Can you imagine how much money is spent on diet pills and other so-called quick fixes? It's phenomenal: billions. But since the average commitment span isn't very long, when things aren't as easy or don't work as anticipated, many throw in the towel and head for the next big thing. They end up losing out on what could have been good, their quitting mentalities foiling their efforts.

One of the only relatively sure bets in life is right in front of you—it's called TODAY. If you're engrossed in reading and absorbing this right now, you're in the present. You're experiencing today.

If you're concerned about one or more aspects of the way your life is going and want change, choose today. Focus on what you can do *today* that will contribute to a better today *and* it'll turn into a better tomorrow. Take steps forward *today* that are on track to achieving your desired objectives. Plan what you will do *today*, and take the first action to get yourself up and running. Now is the time you know you have, and the opportunity to do something positive is now. Procrastination is the sure way to dash your dreams. Staying in the grind without venturing out guarantees an ordinary life. Is that what you want? As you're reading this book say, "Yes" to a brighter future. Get excited about it!

Far too many focus on things that have happened to them in the past, reliving mentally and emotionally what's already done. Rather than their successes, they remember bad breaks, life treating them unfairly, disappointment, failing, and no. They believe that since it happened before, it'll happen again. They continue with the same negative perceptions that brought them to their current dilemma. They excuse themselves from doing the things necessary to reach their casually stated but sometimes deeply rooted objectives, blaming circumstances and people. They surrender to failure without giving success a chance. How sad.

> *"Nothing stops the man who desires to achieve. Every obstacle is simply a course to develop his achievement muscle. It strengthens his power of accomplishment."*
> —ERIC BUTTERWORTH

Dwelling on the past never changes it or creates the future we'd like to have. Have you noticed that? No matter how smart you are or how successful you've become, you can't go back and undo what was done, regardless of whether you perceive it in a positive or negative light. You can, however, be thankful for how it caused you to grow, and choose to see the good in it. You can forgive what and who needs to be forgiven, and also yourself and anything you may regret you did or didn't do. Do this for yourself; it helps you get beyond it all. Go forward and make it better by focusing on the next level of whatever you're pursuing. You can upgrade your knowledge and attitude, taking alternative actions the next time, but you can never change what has already happened. If you don't like what happened in the past, why would you want to dwell on it? Why bother? Learn from it, yes, and move on.

You can't control everything that happens, but you can handle it, asking for help as needed. You can deal with situations in a firm, fair, frank, and friendly manner. You can exert restraint to avoid reactive temper incidents with whatever chill time and forethought is needed to appropriately respond. You can certainly plan for the future, map out your journey, and commit to all you are going to do.

But can you guarantee you'll even be around? Of course not. None of us can. While a better future is your goal, you can't spend any time there until it becomes the present. Each now moment properly invested can make your present flourish instead of wilt and die. Make each second count, for what you do with it helps define your minutes, hours, days, years, and your lifetime.

Plan for a brighter future, learn from the past, but live and control your attitude and behavior today. Today is the time of choice. You can choose to spend your time wisely, or simply enjoy yourself escaping through distractions—wasting your precious time. A life of poorly utilized time is a life of discontent. Who wants that? Not me. How about you? What are you doing with your time? Are you employing it to maximize your momentum toward results you'll be happy with later, or are you frittering it away?

The choice is yours. Make your life one of climbing magnificent mountains. Grab hold of today, and live it better than you did yesterday. If you're blessed enough to have tomorrow, today will be in the past as soon as you wake up. Make your past well worth remembering! Smooth out the bumps with extra consideration and kindness. Surprise those around you!

Focus on what you can control, such as how you proceed today *regardless* of what might happen. You'll eliminate many of the regrets that may have been bothering you deep down. Once again, go with what you have, right where you are, giving it your all. Create a better future—great todays that have yet to happen! Sure, challenges and noes are in the mix—they are for all of us, no matter how unruffled things may look on the surface. You'll get used to them and delight in overcoming them. It'll be as automatic as brushing your teeth. You'll no longer gloss over or avoid dealing with them, because you know that won't get you anywhere. Unfinished business will be a thing of the past.

Waking up with nothing but marvelous potential in front of you is a tremendous way to start the day. Let go of the past. Soften your heart with a true sense of caring and helpfulness. Have a surrendering, ever flowing forgiveness for yourself as an imperfect human being, as well as for others. What if no one ever forgave you for the mistakes you've made? Wouldn't that be a rough state to be in? We have no idea how many people forgive us every day for our oversights, perceived wrongs, or blind sidedness. Thank goodness there are people who have compassion and understanding. It hurts you the most when you hang on to a grievance. The other person(s) may be oblivious to what they said or did, or might have totally forgotten it!

Diligently work to mold your future by molding your todays. Positive words and actions, when incorporated into our daily agenda, add up and can go a long way toward a better life. It's a moment-by-moment process. Make today a day to travel further along your journey, rather than one where you just look back at where you've been. Don't let the future unfold to where you feel you could have done much better had you really applied yourself. You *can* make it happen. Do it today.

Next year is now!

"I have fought the good fight, I have finished the course, I have kept the faith."

—THE APOSTLE PAUL (2 TIMOTHY 4:7)

21

One More Thing...

Creativity is at the core of effective writing which is honed by rewriting, over and over again. To stay fresh and sharp there must be an openness of mind and heart. It facilitates a constant flow of creativity.

Even when they're not working on a book or a newspaper or magazine article, writers consistently exercise their creativity. For me, reading serves as a creative stimulus. I'm a voracious reader. I absolutely love to read. Sometimes it's just simply to enjoy the story. Other times it's to broaden my understanding and knowledge or to specifically explore and reflect on how another writer creates characters, weaves the narrative and dialogue, sets a mood, describes a setting, or teaches a life lesson.

Another thing I enjoy is discovering writing that moves me—that helps me shift my thinking and attitude. It may be soul-shaking, a wake-up call, propelling me to get myself going in the right direction. And, of course, as you may suspect, I like studying the words and the way they were put together and used to affect me in a positive fashion. It all brings me closer to the essence of the writer's intention for the readers. The joy of reading exactly what I need at exactly the time I need it the most is one of the many miracles of being an avid reader. Here's an example of what I mean.

As I work on writing the last few pages of a book, I often get stuck. I think part of it is not wanting to finish something I've worked on for a while, having grown attached to it. Another reason is because I want the end to be and feel just as important as the beginning and the middle. So whenever I get stuck, I read.

Today, I found this wonderful piece...

Your Best Foot Forward

"Which sounds longer to you, 569,400 hours or 65 years? They are exactly the same length of time. The average man spends his first eighteen years—157,000 hours—getting an education. That leaves him 412,000 hours from age 18 to 65. Eight hours of every day are spent in sleeping; eight hours in eating and recreation. One third of the 412,000 hours is 134,000 hours—the number of hours a man has in which to work between the ages of 18 and 65.

Expressed in hours, it doesn't seem like a very long time, does it? Now I am not recommending that you tick off the hours that you worked, 134,000, 133,999, 133,998, etc., but I do suggest whatever you do, do it with all that you have in you. If you are sleeping, sleep well. If you are playing, play well. If you are working, give the best that is in you, remembering that in the final analysis the real satisfactions in life come not from money and things, but from the realization of a job well done. Therein lies the difference between the journeyman worker and a real craftsman."

—H.W. Prentis, Jr.

There Are Two Kinds of People in the World

When I was growing up the world was divided. There were those who lived in big houses and took great vacations. They were "The Haves." Then there were people like my family. Dad worked; Mom made do, stretching every dollar until it hurt. While we never went hungry, we did do without some things. We were part of "The Have Nots."

Fortunately, things changed. My father worked his way up in a company, then risked everything and bought it. For the next twenty-some years he grew it to be one of the oldest, most respected companies in his field. We started taking vacations; Christmas was a little more crowded under the tree; the daily pressure of making ends meet had disappeared. We had become one of "The Haves."

But after years of being told and believing I was destined to be either one or the other, I found it to be a lie—at least partially so. Yes, there are two types of people in the world, but "The Have Nots" aren't one of them.

I break them down as follows: First, yes, there are "The Haves"—those who are where they want to be. Through hard work and an appreciative attitude, they're able to enjoy a rich, fulfilling life.

> *"The successful man will profit from his mistakes and do it again in a different way."*
>
> —DALE CARNEGIE

The other group is in a situation where they are struggling financially. They may not be earning what they need or haven't saved enough to have what they want. They could be in a lot of debt because they chose to have now and pay later. But, in any case, they aren't pleased with where they are.

I call this group, "The Have Tos."

These people still "have to" work toward a goal. Fortunately, they can acquire what they want if their desire is intense enough, if they choose to work for it and stride boldly forward toward it. If these components aren't actively alive and in place, they really shouldn't complain; they certainly shouldn't compare themselves with "The Haves." There's no point in it if they've decided to acquiesce to the status quo and don't care enough to gear themselves up to become one of "The Haves."

For those who fall into "The Have Tos" category, acquiescing to the situation, consider that you aren't going to be around forever. Put the hammer down and vigorously go for the dreams and goals you've been putting on the back burner. This could well be the opportunity of a lifetime to create the air of anticipation and adventure that may now be missing in your life.

That they haven't done the work is reason enough *not* to allow "The Have Nots" to complain. The reality is, the only thing keeping them from what they want is that they "Have To" work to get there. The great news is once they get in motion doing what they "Have To," they can work toward becoming one of "The Haves."

Filled with the Excitement of the Unknown

This is it. We're about to say goodbye for awhile. That you read this lets me know I potentially touched at least one person's life with *Yes!* One person who now refuses to let no stop his or her quest. The effort was worth it! I'm humbled you took the time to let me share my thoughts with you. Until now, that wasn't a sure thing.

As I type these final paragraphs, I can't say for sure that this manuscript will be published. After countless hours over days, weeks, and months, I still can't be sure this will ever be more than words taking up space on my hard drive.

Of course, after having had a number of other books published you might think the odds are in my favor, and they are. But, in publishing, even favorable odds equal a long shot. Every year, over 400,000 new books are published! But less than 1 percent will stick around long enough to make any significant impact.

In spite of those long odds, it was worth every word. As I wrote and imagined where this book was going, I thought about you. I wrote it with one intention—that you would be a bit better off because you read it. I hope this is the case.

As usually follows, there will be engagements tied in with the book. Here is where I ask for something in return. If I'm fortunate enough to speak at an event you're attending, please introduce yourself. Let me know if what I've done has made a difference to you.

Now, I can rest my mind for awhile. Then, it's on to another book. Who knows, maybe it'll be a blockbuster! In the meantime, my desire is that lives are changed, and that I get to meet some people who become more successful because they really understand the importance of no, grow through it, and keep going for yes. That would be an awesome reward. I'm starting to get excited. How about you?

> *"Accept the challenges, so that you may feel the exhilaration of victory."*
>
> —GENERAL GEORGE S. PATTON

Yes! The road to yes is paved with no, and no is for you to grow. As much as we'd all like to avoid it, no is the only thing that prepares us for yes. Remember, it's the yeses that shape your future. No is the proving ground for success. Remember, there's no exit for Easy Street on the highway to your dream.

Now just keep driving, putting on the miles, growing through the noes—racking up the yeses as you achieve whatever it is you're seeking. That's what I'm doing, and if I can do it, anybody can!

Yes!—The Poem

"As I started my quest in search of yes,
I soon found myself rejected by no.
Little did I realize that was the best,
That no was there for me to grow.

I learned not to take no personally,
Even though to me it never felt good.
I discovered that no really strengthened me,
The only thing going that actually would.

I kept pressing on in spite of it all,
And eventually the yeses they came.
I kept pressing on in spite of it all,
And I've never been just quite the same.

I grew and overcame my fears alright,
Of others not choosing to join the quest.
I knew that as long as I kept going bright,
I'd surely in time find only the best.

So never give up as you follow your dream,
No matter how hard it may oftentimes seem.
For it never quite matters how many resist,
The victory goes only to those who persist.

Yes, noes are for you to prosper and grow,
As you move on to what you are after.
The yeses will come and you surely will know,
They are what count the most ever after.

If only I'd known earlier to go and seek no,
I would have grown faster and sooner got yes.
So now that I'm sure of the power of no,
I'm getting more yeses and untold success."

—The Editors at *Possibility Press*

Who Is John Fuhrman?

An award-winning sales producer and manager, John Fuhrman is a speaker, peak-performance trainer, and consultant for Fortune 100 companies and other organizations. He is committed to encouraging others and helping them enhance their performance professionally and personally.

John's messages are based on his business and personal life experiences, and well as his years as a dedicated trainer. Since 1996, he has helped over a million people, around the globe, through his books and live performances. He speaks and writes with a special sensitivity for helping people grow themselves, their careers and businesses, while striving for their objectives.

He is sought after as a speaker and author on rejection, sales, success, motivation, and e-commerce, as well as on sales, leadership, debt reduction, and wealth creation. He can be reached at rejectme@aol.com.